Building Educator Capacity Through Microcredentials

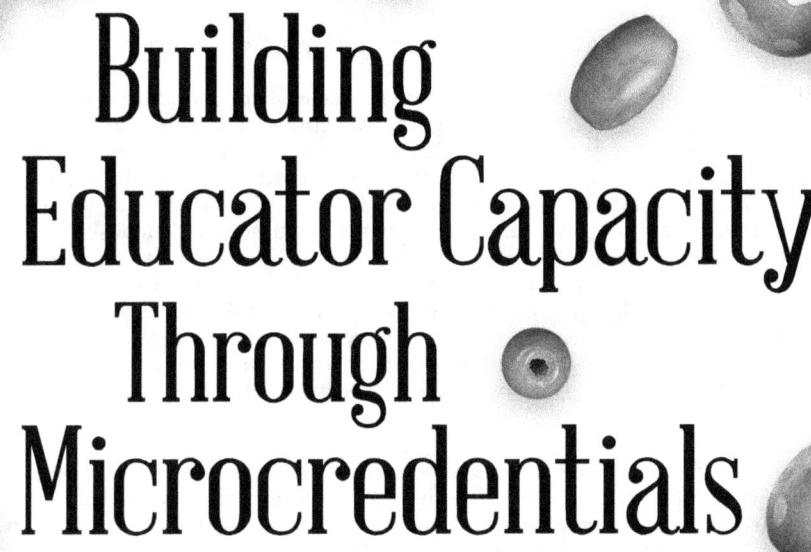

Building Educator Capacity Through Microcredentials

Eric M. Carbaugh
Laura McCullough
Meghan Raftery
Ebbie Linaburg

Arlington, Virginia USA

2800 Shirlington Road, Suite 1001 • Arlington, VA 22206 USA
Phone: 800-933-2723 or 703-578-9600 • Fax: 703-575-5400
Website: www.ascd.org • Email: member@ascd.org
Author guidelines: www.ascd.org/write

Penny Reinart, *Chief Impact Officer*; Genny Ostertag, *Managing Director, Book Acquisitions & Editing*; Allison Scott, *Senior Acquisitions Editor*; Julie Houtz, *Director, Book Editing*; Liz Wegner, *Editor*; Thomas Lytle, *Creative Director*; Donald Ely, *Art Director*; Georgia Park, *Senior Graphic Designer*; Keith Demmons, *Senior Production Designer*; Kelly Marshall, *Production Manager*; Shajuan Martin, *E-Publishing Specialist*; Christopher Logan, *Senior Production Specialist*

Copyright © 2022 ASCD. All rights reserved. It is illegal to reproduce copies of this work in print or electronic format (including reproductions displayed on a secure intranet or stored in a retrieval system or other electronic storage device from which copies can be made or displayed) without the prior written permission of the publisher. By purchasing only authorized electronic or print editions and not participating in or encouraging piracy of copyrighted materials, you support the rights of authors and publishers. Readers who wish to reproduce or republish excerpts of this work in print or electronic format may do so for a small fee by contacting the Copyright Clearance Center (CCC), 222 Rosewood Dr., Danvers, MA 01923, USA (phone: 978-750-8400; fax: 978-646-8600; web: www.copyright.com). To inquire about site licensing options or any other reuse, contact ASCD Permissions at www.ascd.org/permissions or permissions@ascd.org. For a list of vendors authorized to license ASCD e-books to institutions, see www.ascd.org/epubs. Send translation inquiries to translations@ascd.org.

ASCD® is a registered trademark of Association for Supervision and Curriculum Development. All other trademarks contained in this book are the property of, and reserved by, their respective owners, and are used for editorial and informational purposes only. No such use should be construed to imply sponsorship or endorsement of the book by the respective owners.

All web links in this book are correct as of the publication date below but may have become inactive or otherwise modified since that time. If you notice a deactivated or changed link, please email books@ascd.org with the words "Link Update" in the subject line. In your message, please specify the web link, the book title, and the page number on which the link appears.

PAPERBACK ISBN: 978-1-4166-3133-0   ASCD product #123013   n8/22
PDF E-BOOK ISBN: 978-1-4166-3134-7; see Books in Print for other formats.
Quantity discounts are available: email programteam@ascd.org or call 800-933-2723, ext. 5773, or 703-575-5773. For desk copies, go to www.ascd.org/deskcopy.

Library of Congress Cataloging-in-Publication Data
Names: Carbaugh, Eric M., author. | McCullough, Laura L., 1954- author. |
  Raftery, Meghan, author. | Linaburg, Ebbie, author.
Title: Building educator capacity through microcredentials / Eric M.
  Carbaugh, Laura McCullough, Meghan Raftery, and Ebbie Linaburg.
Description: Arlington, VA : ASCD, 2022. | Includes bibliographical
  references and index.
Identifiers: LCCN 2022011327 (print) | LCCN 2022011328 (ebook) | ISBN
  9781416631330 (paperback) | ISBN 9781416631347 (pdf)
Subjects: LCSH: Teachers--Education (Continuing education)--United States.
  | Teachers--In-service training--United States. |
  Microcredentials--United States.
Classification: LCC LB1715 .C3218 2022 (print) | LCC LB1715 (ebook) | DDC
  370.71/1--dc23/eng/20220603
LC record available at https://lccn.loc.gov/2022011327
LC ebook record available at https://lccn.loc.gov/2022011328

---

31 30 29 28 27 26 25 24 23 22   1 2 3 4 5 6 7 8 9 10 11 12

Building Educator Capacity Through Microcredentials

Acknowledgments vii

Introduction: Why Microcredentials? 1

1. The Intersection of Microcredentials and
   High-Quality Professional Learning 11

2. Meeting School and District Goals 25

3. Selecting Microcredentials 41

4. Designing Microcredentials 55

5. Implementing a Microcredentialing Process 73

6. Leading for Success 87

Conclusion 99

Appendix A: Microcredential Key Traits Checklist 101

Appendix B: Virginia Beach City Public Schools
   Social Awareness Badge Criteria 105

Appendix C: Microcredential Criteria Checklist for Designers 107

Appendix D: Annotated Microcredential 111

Appendix E: Microcredential Reviewers Checklist 117

References 121

Index 125

About the Authors 129

Acknowledgments

Our understanding of microcredentials and our ability to design and implement them as tools for professional learning began at an ASCD conference session with Sue Z. Beers, now executive director of *MISIC: Members Impacting Students; Improving Curriculum* in Iowa. That conference session sparked a series of conversations, training for our microcredential designers, numerous phone and Zoom calls, and a lasting friendship. We would not have embarked on this project had she not encouraged us. Many of the ideas found here originated with Sue—we thank her for both her inspiration and practical advice. Sue can be reached at suebeers@netins.net.

Introduction: Why Microcredentials?

Educators know a great deal about how people learn. We know that the most powerful learning experiences—the ones that "stick"—are authentic and competency-based. They occur in a real-world context and are designed to have learners demonstrate *what they know* by showing *what they can do*. We understand that learners vary in their background knowledge, skills, and interests, so instruction should be personalized to meet diverse and rapidly changing needs. We know that hearing a lecture (even an interesting one!) does not equip learners with either deep understanding or competence in a skill. Despite these understandings, professional learning for educators rarely reflects these ideas. It is more likely to be standardized than personalized, often involves listening to or observing experts rather than engaging in active learning, is typically uncoupled from rather than embedded in educators' everyday practice, and seldom includes demonstrations of professional competency.

A variety of professional learning strategies and models are needed to completely close this gap between what we know about learning and how we apply it to our practice. We believe that microcredentialing is one of the key strategies for doing so. In this book, we describe how microcredentials provide opportunities for flexibility, personalization, engagement, and self-direction on the part of the learner. We argue that, when designed according to quality criteria, the process of earning microcredentials occurs *within* the context of educators' professional roles rather than *apart* from it.

We wrote this book because, in the process of designing and implementing microcredentials over the past two years, we have come to believe that well-designed, high-quality microcredentials are powerful tools for both professional learning and documentation of complex, transferable skills that benefit student learning, moving educators from simply saying "I get it" to asserting "I have evidence it transformed my students."

Over the past several years, we have advocated for modernizing curriculum and instruction to provide students with learning experiences that are more relevant to their lives, more personalized, and more project- and performance-based. We believe that students' ability to demonstrate their competence matters more than their seat time in a class. As we've watched teachers design and use meaningful, performance-based assessments with students, we've seen students engage with open-ended tasks, using clear performance criteria to strengthen and document their skills. And we have wondered, don't our teachers deserve access to these same kinds of transferable, meaningful, and transformational learning experiences?

Competency Versus Seat Time

How do we know when we are good at something? Does having 45 contact hours with your professor prove that you learned something of value? Should 180 days of school attendance be accepted as evidence of success? Of course, we know that time is not a measure of learning, but rather a variable. Each of us has our own prior experience and background knowledge, so we are at different starting points and will progress at different rates when learning something new.

Like Carnegie Units for students, professional learning credits are often awarded to teachers based on the number of hours spent at a conference or workshop without regard for what is learned, how it is applied, or who is affected. But we realize that all the teachers who attended that eight-hour conference did not start with the same experience or learn at the same rate. Further, the fact that they spent time in a session, whether in person or online, tells us nothing about any associated change in practice that might benefit their students in some way. Back at school in their classrooms, they may or may not apply their learning to practice.

Microcredentialing, by contrast, is a competency-based approach to professional learning. That is, the learning goal is a skill that can be documented through observation or other evidence. Determining the degree to which learners have met one or more competencies is generally done through performance-based assessments within the context of their work. After all, we don't issue driver's licenses without behind-the-wheel testing or determine students' writing proficiency without examining their writing. In the same way, educators can use the structure of microcredentials to demonstrate their proficiency in various skills (competencies) that are important to their effectiveness.

Those of us who grew up in Boy Scouts or Girl Scouts are familiar with the process of earning badges. We learned background information and applied it to a skill. We then practiced that skill and demonstrated it to earn our badges, which signified our proficiency. Credentials that document evidence of proficiency—versus credits earned, points accumulated, or hours spent—lend credibility to a résumé or professional portfolio and provide information about an individual's particular skill set. Evidence submitted for a microcredential is examined by trained assessors, who compare it to a set of criteria described on a rubric. If the evidence meets the criteria, the microcredential is awarded. In some systems, multiple microcredentials are "stacked" or "bundled" together to indicate proficiency in a broader skill area or in greater depth. Not only do microcredentials provide a method for documenting skills, they also capture the teacher's depth of understanding and ability to reflect on practice. When teachers are developing and demonstrating complex, higher-level competencies, microcredentials are especially appropriate.

This book addresses characteristics of high-quality microcredentials in detail, including guidelines for choosing them, models for designing them, examples, and implementation strategies. But before considering those specifics, it's important to focus attention on a few ideas that have driven our work.

Completing a microcredential is not the quickest or easiest way to earn continuing education credits, relicensure, or certification. Most teachers describe their experience with microcredentials as rigorous—not simply more or harder work, but work that is intellectually challenging, meaningful, and relevant. Often, they see their efforts reflected in the quality of their students' work and the level of student engagement. The experience is worthwhile for teachers when they acquire a skill that strengthens their teaching and, in turn, has a positive effect on student learning.

We believe that the following basic traits are necessary ingredients of any successful microcredentialing process:

1. **They are performance-based.** Like all well-designed performance assessments, microcredentials require learners to "show what they know," transferring their understanding into a demonstration of competence that positively affects student outcomes.
2. **They are flexible and self-directed.** Because microcredentials are self-directed, teachers can choose resources, supports, and learning pathways that best meet their needs as they prepare to demonstrate their proficiency. In addition, microcredentials are flexible: in many cases, they assess skills that can be applied across a variety of grade levels, content specialties, and teaching situations.
3. **They are contextual.** Research has consistently shown that the most effective professional learning is job-embedded (Darling-Hammond et al., 2017). Earning a microcredential not only provides the opportunity for job-embedded work but requires it.

We'll have more to say about these traits, as well as additional characteristics of high-quality microcredentials, in Chapter 1.

Meeting the Needs of Teachers, Schools, and Districts

Beyond their benefits for individual teachers, microcredentials offer a number of advantages for schools and districts. High-quality microcredentials reflect research-based practices for effective professional learning, embedding those practices in performance-based assessments that turn theory into observable action. They offer flexibility and personalization for users while defining clear success criteria, allowing schools and school districts to use them to build capacity across organizations while providing differentiated and personalized learning opportunities for educators. Microcredentials have specific skills and learning targets that require transferring learning into practice. A professional learning plan that incorporates microcredentials clarifies the intended outcomes ahead of time, enabling individual teachers, schools, or districts to match microcredentials to their needs.

We are proponents of invigorating and practical "one and done" professional learning experiences like conferences and workshops. We know that exposure to experts and sharing of ideas among educators are helpful in developing thinking about theory and practice, and we consider these experiences to be valuable jumping-off points for meaningful professional learning. However, relying on these models alone rarely influences practice in any meaningful way. Some form of follow-up or application in context is necessary to make the learning stick (Ende, 2021). Microcredentials build this application phase into their design, serving as performance-based assessments of professional skills and substantially increasing the odds that educators' professional learning will positively affect student learning.

Like individual teachers, schools and districts use data to identify areas for growth. School improvement plans and district strategic plans generally define focus areas for improvement, and too often this translates into canned or scripted professional learning programs that are required for all staff. But we assume that not all educators start from the same place. Like their students, they have varying levels of prior knowledge, differing experiences, and distinct modes of learning. Microcredentials offer the flexibility of multiple starting points and choices in learning pathways, even as all participants are growing their skills in the same area of expertise. This "standardized but personalized" nature of microcredentials creates a shared knowledge base, language, and foundation for meeting school or district goals.

We are fortunate to have relationships with school districts, states, and organizations that are using microcredentials to meet districtwide goals. Each of the following entities is implementing microcredentialing for different purposes and in different ways, yet they all illustrate the benefits of this approach for building capacity and documenting competency among teachers:

- **Albemarle County Public Schools, Virginia.** Located in central Virginia, Albemarle serves more than 14,000 students in prekindergarten through 12th grade (Albemarle County Public Schools, 2021a). The district offers several microcredentials that are housed within different district offices. In this book, we examine Albemarle's work related to

culturally responsive teaching, which aligns with its district equity and anti-racism policies.
- **Los Angeles Unified School District, California.** Spanning 720 square miles across Southern California, Los Angeles Unified is the second-largest school district in the United States, serving over 600,000 students in more than 1,000 schools, including 200 independently operated public charter schools (Los Angeles Unified School District, 2021). The district is piloting a cohort focused on project-based learning (PBL) called "PBL Champions," which will complete 15 hours of in-person instruction and 30 hours of job-embedded learning, both supported by the completion of nine microcredentials. When participants earn their PBL "medallion," they can choose to redeem it for increased compensation.
- **Members Impacting Students; Improving Curriculum (MISIC), Iowa.** MISIC is a nonprofit consortium serving 75 member school districts in Iowa. The consortium provides curriculum resources, technical assistance, and professional learning, including an extensive catalog of microcredentials, to educators in member districts. MISIC's pioneering work in microcredential design and implementation has provided direction and insight to designers across the country.
- **Norwalk Public Schools, Connecticut.** Located in southern Connecticut, Norwalk Public Schools serves 11,700 students across 21 schools (Norwalk Public Schools, 2021). The district is piloting a stack of microcredentials created by an outside company with one high school focused on project-based learning. The credentials will be used to create a "résumé" for each teacher.
- **Richardson Independent School District (ISD), Texas.** Richardson ISD is located just north of Dallas and enrolls approximately 40,000 students (Texas Education Agency, 2020). The district offers 12 microcredentials, or "badges," on a variety of topics—some developed in house or locally and others outsourced farther afield. Microcredentials are tied to teacher compensation and are supported by district leader coaches for each topic. Teachers choose how many microcredentials they would like to complete.
- **Davis School District, Farmington, Utah.** An initiative by Davis School District in Farmington, near Salt Lake City, to use microcredentials

for personalized and competency-based professional learning led to a collaboration with the Utah State Board of Education known as Utah Microcredentials, which in turn resulted in the state's microcredentialing process for adding endorsements and earning USBE credits for relicensure.
- **Virginia Beach City Public Schools, Virginia.** Located on the eastern coast of the state, Virginia Beach City Public Schools serves around 63,000 students in kindergarten through 12th grade (Virginia Beach City Public Schools, 2021). The district has been working for several years to define teacher "specializations" related to the district strategic plan, including in topics like personalized learning and social-emotional learning. The specializations are developed with and for teacher teams that also pilot the microcredentials.
- **Winchester Public Schools, Virginia.** Located in northwestern Virginia, this district serves approximately 4,300 students in prekindergarten through 12th grade (Winchester Public Schools, 2021). Winchester Public Schools is using microcredentials from outside companies to provide training in computer science to elementary teachers as they implement a grant.

Throughout this book, you'll read vignettes "from the field" showing the ways that these organizations have designed and implemented their approaches to microcredentialing and the impact their efforts have had.

Our Path to Microcredentials

The four of us have different jobs, perspectives, and experiences in education. Our paths crossed though our involvement in VASCD, the Virginia affiliate of ASCD. Eric is a professor working with preservice teachers at James Madison University and an ASCD Faculty member; Ebbie is a recently retired assistant superintendent; Meghan is chief design officer of the Edjacent Design Collaborative; and Laura has recently retired from her post as executive director of VASCD. Though we come to our microcredentialing work from different perspectives, we also have common values and interests. All of us are advocates for teachers, proponents of deep thinking about teaching and learning, and designers of performance-based assessment. We are believers in *autonomy with integrity*; we know that teachers are principled and wise, and that given the freedom to make choices about their professional learning, they will prioritize their students' needs as the driver of their decisions.

Using This Book

This book serves as an introduction to microcredentials for those who simply want to understand what they are and how they work, but we have other aims as well. Our intention is for educators who are exploring microcredentials for their districts, schools, or themselves as individuals to use the guidelines and examples we provide as measures of quality. For those who desire to build their own customized microcredentials to advance specific learning targets in their organizations, we provide templates and design tips. Readers who may already be using microcredentials will also find implementation advice. Just as we advocate for professionals using microcredentials to choose their own learning paths, we invite you to choose and use our content to the extent and in the sequence that is most helpful in your context.

In Chapter 1, we describe how microcredentials reflect what we know about effective professional learning. We propose defining characteristics—the criteria we look for in high-quality microcredentials. We also describe some of the ways that microcredentials differ from one another and the implications of those differences.

In Chapter 2, we suggest an approach to microcredential implementation that reflects the ways we plan for deep and meaningful learning. We describe how to begin with a theory of action that leads to overarching goals, using research to choose the most impactful microcredentials and ensuring personalized learning pathways aligned to those goals. An implementation plan that is thoughtfully developed will ensure that users have a meaningful learning experience and a good chance of success.

Microcredentials for educators are widely available, though they may or may not fit the needs of your school or district. Maybe you're thinking of designing your own. In Chapter 3, we provide guidelines for deciding whether to adopt or design and suggest factors to consider when choosing microcredentials from an outside provider.

Should you determine that designing your own microcredentials is the correct path, as we have over the past two years, Chapter 4 outlines a design process and offers tips about quality criteria as well as providing a series of design questions based on our experiences and those of the school districts profiled in this book.

Beyond the obvious benefit to individuals, approaching microcredentialing with organizational purposes in mind can maximize their impact. High-quality microcredentials are becoming more widely available. They are offered by professional associations and other nonprofits, institutions of higher education, and for-profit companies. Chapter 5 provides guidance for implementing microcredentials whether they are from providers or designed by a school or district. Finally, Chapter 6 examines the vital role that leadership plays in structuring and supporting microcredentialing at scale.

A competency-based approach allows learning and assessment to complement each other. As one teacher who completed one of our microcredentials said, "I do a lot of work around assessment for learning, and this microcredential project is a perfect example of such assessment. We [my co-teacher and I] learned so much and were so inspired by the growth we saw in our students as all of us worked through the activities of the project." Our hope is that as educators continue to explore the potential of transformational competency-based professional learning, they will discover connections to teacher evaluation and licensure that truly represent assessment of *and* for learning within our profession.

1

The Intersection of Microcredentials and High-Quality Professional Learning

Like any professional learning resource, microcredentials should be selected and designed with attention to quality criteria. In this chapter, we highlight some of the most important elements of effective professional learning, demonstrate how microcredentials can reflect these elements, and provide guidance on what to look for in a high-quality microcredential. We also point out some of the ways in which microcredential designs vary, even among those that satisfy our quality criteria.

Effective Professional Learning

Although researchers don't always agree on the specific elements of effective professional learning, they do agree on how *effectiveness* should be defined. Most concur that professional learning is effective when it has a positive and "enduring impact" on school leadership, classroom practice, and student learning. In this context, student learning includes not only academic achievement, but also behavioral outcomes such as attendance, engagement, and dropout rates and affective goals related to social-emotional learning (Guskey, 2021).

The evidence for effectiveness of traditional professional learning is thin. As Jacob and McGovern (2015) write, "We bombard teachers with help, but most of it is not helpful—to teachers as professionals or to schools seeking better instruction" (p. 4). A great deal of what teachers may learn in settings like conferences and workshops never transfers into their practice (Joyce &

Showers, 2002), so it cannot have the enduring impact that Guskey describes above.

There is no single formula for effective professional learning. Like any learning, it relies on a range of variables, such as the educator's prior knowledge and current practice, the characteristics of the students and community, and the culture of the school. Professional learning is complex and dependent on the interaction of many factors. However, both research and experience suggest that the following characteristics, when built into professional learning designs, increase their effectiveness.

Learning Is Goal-Oriented

Like any effective instruction, professional learning should begin with the end in mind—and that end, of course, is value for students. Designers and providers of professional learning should ensure that there is a through line to intended student learning goals, whether academic or social-emotional. It's reasonable to conclude that a teacher will more likely connect professional learning to actual practice if there is a clear, achievable goal predicted to positively affect students. Camp (2017) suggests that teacher goal setting "has the potential to benefit teachers through providing a lens through which to scrutinize their teaching and the opportunity to chart their own path toward learning and improvement" (p. 70). Goal-oriented microcredentials provide a path to a specific professional learning target.

Learning Is a Process Rather Than an Event

The advantage of professional learning experiences that are sustained over time is clear. Conferences and workshops lasting 14 hours or less show no statistically significant effect on student learning (Wei et al., 2009). This is not to suggest that conferences or workshops are not valuable—they can provide access to ideas and experts that otherwise would not be available. (In fact, a conference session inspired our own foray into microcredentialing!) They can also frame important problems of practice within schools and provide context for deeper learning. But alone, they do not constitute high-value professional learning. Rather, they are important components of a learning *process*. What happens before and after such events is essential to determining the extent to which the learning is transferred into practice. Educators need time to experiment, practice, and receive feedback. Professional learning community work, peer observation, and other forms of collaboration can be combined with a conference experience to produce powerful learning. Microcredentials provide a structure for sustained work over time.

Learning Is Job-Embedded and Relevant

Though a professional learning plan may include a graduate course, a book study, a webinar, or a conference, deeper learning happens through application and feedback. Webster-Wright (2009) contrasts professional development that is "delivered" with professional learning that is experienced in a more authentic, situated way:

> In seeking a way forward to support professionals in their continuing learning, guidelines are required that are congruent with professionals' authentic experiences of learning, yet cognizant of the realities of the workplace with respect to professional responsibilities. Constructive strategies need to be developed to enable change from the current practice of delivering [professional development] to that of supporting authentic [professional learning]. (p. 726)

Most educators can describe times they've left a professional development session wondering how it related to their work—or convinced that it didn't relate to it at all. Practitioners value professional learning when they can see evidence with their own students in their own classrooms that something is working. To that end, educators should earn microcredentials by collecting evidence from their daily work with students.

Learning Is Personalized

Educators need to have a voice in their professional learning. Even when the goals of a school or division require that all staff build their capacity in a specific area, leaders should give thought to differentiation and choice about *how* to learn, so that these experiences can still be personalized. Marker and Watson (2018) note that when given the autonomy to design their professional learning plans, "teachers created meaningful learning experiences that changed their individual practices and affected the greater community" (para. 2). A group of teachers or even an entire faculty can be working toward the same microcredential while each individual creates a learning pathway unique to his or her needs.

As we shift our work with students away from a focus on memorization and seat time and toward more meaningful and engaging experiences, we can and must do the same for teachers and school leaders. It is essential that our professional learning models be goal-oriented, processes rather than discrete events, job-embedded, and personalized. When carefully designed, they can incorporate all these features, increasing the odds that professional learning will stick with the teacher and transfer into practice that benefits students.

Defining Microcredentials

What exactly *is* a microcredential? The answer to this question depends on whom you ask. Because there is no widely accepted organization for accrediting microcredentials, the definition is whatever the awarding entity says it is. In some cases, earning a microcredential is as simple as completing a set of readings and passing a test at the end of an online module. The term *microcredential* can mean almost anything, which is one reason we believe this book is so important. Consider these responses to the question "How do you define microcredentials?" from education leaders:

- Lars Holmstrom, Albemarle: "A microcredential, in Albemarle, means a system through which educators are validating their learning, application, and impact on student outcomes in a focused area" (personal communication, June 25, 2021).
- Tina Henckel, Norwalk: "A microcredential is a series of professional development opportunities teachers engage in to be a leader in [a given] area" (personal communication, June 17, 2021).
- Utah Microcredentials: "A microcredential, also known as a badge, is a digital form of certification indicating demonstrated competency/mastery of a specific skill through evidence of planning/preparation, implementation, and reflection" (Utah Microcredentials, 2021).
- Tabitha Branum, Richardson: "It means to us that you have engaged in a series of learning experiences that in the end lead you to a defined outcome. The outcome might be a learning objective, a skillset, an artifact—some kind of outcome we've identified, and you've engaged in PD that led to the outcome" (personal communication, May 21, 2021).

- Janene Gorham, Virginia Beach: "A microcredential is the demonstration of an articulated competency with skills embedded" (personal communication, May 14, 2021).

None of these answers is right or wrong. We share them simply to demonstrate the variability in the ways microcredentials have been defined. We applaud school districts that are using microcredentials to build capacity, meet specific goals, and provide meaningful professional learning experiences. At the same time, we see the advantage in a common definition and shared set of quality criteria. Suppose a teacher moves from one school district to another and brings with them a microcredential they earned the previous year. Without a common definition, the microcredential may have no meaning (or be completely misinterpreted) in the teacher's new assignment.

We define microcredentials as *performance-based assessments intended to allow the educator to demonstrate competency in a skill*. Microcredentials incorporate pathways whereby learning can occur and the skill can be strengthened as the teacher works toward the credentials, making them assessments *for* learning. Like the performance assessments we use with our students, they should include the following essential components:

- Clear learning targets
- Success criteria (which will also be found in the rubric)
- Resources for learning about and preparing for the learning task
- A performance task composed of one or more job-embedded activities and designed to demonstrate the learning targets
- Pre-reflection questions to activate prior knowledge and provide context for the task and post-reflection questions to consider the impact of the performance task on teacher practice and student outcomes
- A description of the evidence that will be used to assess competency

We discuss these essential components further later in this book. For now, consider this outline of a microcredential documenting teacher questioning skills as an example.

Skill: Elicit student thinking at higher cognitive levels through questioning.

1. *Learning targets:*

- Create questions that are aligned with standards.
- Design questions to elicit higher-level thinking that match the higher levels of Bloom's taxonomy or Webb's Depth of Knowledge (DOK).
- Pose questions during the course of a lesson that elicit higher-level thinking from students.
- Describe the connection between types of questions and the thinking revealed in the content of student responses.

2. *Learning resources:*
   - Article: "Depth-of-Knowledge Levels for Four Content Areas" by Norman L. Webb (www.maine.gov/doe/sites/maine.gov.doe/files/inline-files/dok.pdf)
   - Article: "A Revision of Bloom's Taxonomy" by David R. Krathwohl (www.depauw.edu/files/resources/krathwohl.pdf)
   - Article: "Generating Effective Questions" by Todd Finley (www.edutopia.org/blog/new-classroom-questioning-techniques-todd-finley)
   - Video: "Inquiry-Based Teaching: Asking Effective Questions" (https://learn.teachingchannel.com/video/questions-for-inquiry-based-teaching)
   - Article: "Asking Good Questions" (www.ascd.org/el/articles/asking-good-questions)

3. *Task:*
   - Activity 1: Create a lesson plan (using the template of your choice) with pre-planned questions written out for each stage of the learning process. Identify the strategy you will use with each question and the purpose of the question (check for understanding, engage students, deepen student thinking, etc.). The lesson plan needs to include the standard, learning target or targets, activities and strategies, and multiple pre-planned questions designed to elicit higher-level thinking (highlight these on your plan).
   - Activity 2: Make a video recording of yourself implementing this lesson or of a subsequent lesson for which you have planned questions designed to elicit higher-level thinking. As you view your recording, create a list of the questions asked and label each question with a level using either

the revised version of Bloom's taxonomy or Webb's DOK. Include notes describing what you notice about student responses and about your own questioning.
- Activity 3: Write a short narrative in which you analyze your use of questioning in the lesson, describe any impact you see on student responses or learning, and reflect on what adjustments you might make to your strategy for an upcoming lesson in which you will use questioning to elicit student thinking.

4. *Pre- and post-reflections:*
   - Pre: What previous experiences do you have with this concept?
   - Pre: What are some questioning strategies you have found success with? On what would you like to improve?
   - Post: What did you notice about the level of discourse in your classroom? What improved? How do you know?
   - Post: What would you like to continue to improve going forward? What will you continue to do? Why?

5. *Evidence that will be used to assess competency:*
   - Highlighted lesson plan
   - List of questions with labels and your notes
   - Narrative

One additional note about the learning resources. When teachers can select the resources they would like to use to help complete the task, they are crafting their own learning pathway. As a result, the learning pathway associated with a microcredential is personalized; that is, the educator has the autonomy to choose professional learning opportunities to prepare for the assessment. Although resources such as articles, examples, or videos are included in the microcredential, educators may choose additional resources that better meet their learning needs, such as feedback from a colleague, focused work with a coach, or participation in a workshop or course. Some teachers will read the rubric and determine that they are ready to meet the criteria without taking advantage of any of these learning resources. In our model, one of the strengths of microcredentials is that they afford teachers the opportunity for self-directed, personalized learning, and we believe that determining readiness is the prerogative of each individual teacher.

How High-Quality Microcredentials Reflect Effective Professional Learning

As we note in the Introduction, we believe that high-quality microcredentials are *performance-based, flexible/self-directed*, and *contextual*. These traits align to the characteristics of effective professional learning outlined above, in that *performance-based* aligns with *goal-oriented, flexible/self-directed* aligns with *personalized*, and *contextual* aligns with both *a process rather than an event* as well as *job-embedded and relevant*. Knowing these traits is helpful as a starting point for assessing the quality of a microcredential. Here, we provide a bit more detail on each trait and additional criteria for determining the quality of a microcredential.

Performance-Based

A microcredential requires transfer of skills in an authentic context—typically the teacher's daily work. Microcredentials include rubrics that clearly define proficiency and specify criteria that are aligned with the target skills. The microcredential is awarded based on an examination of evidence (often by an external, objective assessor) documenting that the teacher is proficient in the skill as identified in the learning target and described in the rubric. Neither seat time nor clock hours are considered in the assessment of proficiency. Some teachers may be able to earn a microcredential using existing evidence, while others will need extended time for research, practice, or feedback before their evidence is sufficient to meet the rubric criteria.

Contextual

Earning a microcredential means providing evidence of the skill as it is demonstrated in the course of teachers' existing work rather than passing a test or producing a project, paper, or presentation solely for the purpose of meeting a professional learning requirement. When teachers pursue microcredentials, an important part of the work is determining how best to apply the skill to their grade level, content area, and specific group of students.

For example, suppose a 5th grade teacher is working to earn a microcredential in student collaboration. This teacher is interested in building a learning culture in her classroom where students help and learn from each other as they work toward shared goals. She has used structured protocols before for group work and cooperative learning; students have followed directions and been compliant, but their engagement with one another has been mostly perfunctory. Here are some questions the teacher might ask herself as she digs into the microcredential criteria and resources:

- What are the differences between what my students are currently doing and the kind of collaboration described in the microcredential?
- What kind of collaboration might I see that is generally appropriate for my students' developmental levels, reflects my own goals, and aligns with the microcredential's learning targets and success criteria?
- Given what I know about my curriculum and my students, what are the best places and when are the best times for us to work on strengthening collaboration? Where will I embed this in my teaching?
- How will students learn and practice collaboration?
- What resources, support, or feedback would help me as I build my own skill in this area? Where will I access those?
- What is my plan and timeline, and from which units, lessons, or activities will I collect my evidence?

The thinking needed to answer these kinds of planning questions and the reflection and self-assessment that occur after the teacher has collected and examined evidence are important aspects of the microcredentialing process. We have all attended professional learning events that left educators with the perception that, although the presentation might have been interesting, it offered nothing relevant to them or wouldn't work in their school or with their students. Microcredentialing flips this script. Before the work takes place, practitioners have the opportunity—and responsibility—to determine what the skill will look like and where it fits best in their context. We believe that this process of planning, reflection, and decision making is an important aspect of the learning and helps to ensure that skills gained through microcredentialing will become part of the educator's repertoire.

Personalized

The evidence that indicates successful completion of a microcredential must match the rubric's success criteria. In this respect, microcredentials are standardized, but the tasks required are typically open-ended enough to allow for a variety of responses. Consider, for example, the following three scenarios describing teachers who have all enrolled in the same microcredential for implementing peer feedback.

Scenario one: Sofia is a high school science teacher whose students regularly work in small groups to complete labs and research projects. Her students generally work together well and often give each other advice and assistance. Sofia believes student achievement will improve if she incorporates activities in which students' interactions focus specifically on improving their work using the quality criteria found in her rubrics. Sofia has a good idea of what she wants to accomplish as she begins the microcredential, but she's not familiar with protocols or strategies she could teach and have students practice so that their feedback would be focused on the learning targets, delivered in the appropriate way, and seen as helpful by the recipients. She reads three articles and watches a video of a high school teacher implementing peer feedback. She also spends two class periods observing her school's chorus teacher conduct sessions in which students use a selection of rubric criteria to provide feedback to small groups practicing songs for an upcoming concert. Using these resources, she maps out a plan for student-to-student feedback that is an adaptation of the strategies she picked up in her reading and observation and that she believes will be challenging but attainable for her students. Sofia checks her plan to ensure that it will produce the evidence needed for the microcredential, and she is ready to begin.

Scenario two: Justin is a second-year teacher working with 3rd graders. His first year was challenging but successful, and he has started his second year with a degree of confidence about the general structure and strategies around which he will plan his instruction. Justin is motivated to add to his teaching toolbox; he spends much of his spare time reading, collecting ideas from his colleagues at school, and following innovative teachers on social media. Conceptually, he understands the benefits of peer feedback and would like to build the strategy into his writing instruction; he just doesn't know where to begin. So he attends a day-long workshop on teaching writing that includes ways to embed peer feedback. Then, returning to school with some specific ideas, he asks his instructional coach to help him use these strategies in his upcoming lessons. He sees the microcredential as the perfect way to document his new learning and hold himself accountable for integrating it into his practice. Justin can also earn continuing education units (CEUs) for successful completion of the microcredential. (We discuss incentives for completing microcredentials in greater detail in Chapters 5 and 6.)

Scenario three: Marcie teaches computer science to a multigrade group of high school students. As the students' coding skills improve and they build programs using more and more complex algorithms, Marcie routinely has them evaluate one another's programming, pointing out possible errors and working in pairs to test and troubleshoot. She has read the rubric for the microcredential on implementing peer feedback and has reviewed the evidence that needs to be submitted to meet the requirements for completion. Marcie is confident that she can demonstrate her competency in the skill and provide the evidence by simply doing what she would be doing anyway in her next unit—she'll just have to be sure she documents the work in the ways the microcredential specifies. She makes a few notes in her existing lesson plans to remind herself and does not consult any other learning resources. Marcie plans to apply for a position as an instructional coach using her microcredential as part of her portfolio.

All three of these teachers are doing exactly what we would want them to do, even though they are approaching the microcredential in different ways and for different reasons. The forethought that goes into teachers understanding the learning target, envisioning how it would best apply in their classrooms, and then identifying their own learning needs is an important beginning step and results in a different path for each teacher.

The three traits above are essential to meeting our definition of a microcredential. Four additional characteristics, described below, are reflected in microcredentials we would describe as high in quality.

Standardized

In the scenarios above, each of the three teachers takes a different approach to preparing for the microcredential task. The teachers all work in different grade levels, with different content and different students, but the *outcome*—or competency—is the same. Each of them will demonstrate their skill in teaching students to give peer feedback to improve the quality of their work prior to receiving feedback from and being evaluated by the teacher. Standardization assures participants that if they earn the microcredential, they are performing the skill at a solid level of proficiency. Generally, teachers are awarded digital badges or certificates to show that they have earned microcredentials, validating their proficiency in the associated skill. This documentation is also useful when communicating to others, such as in a professional portfolio or as part of a job application. It is essential that the skill is clearly defined and that success criteria are applied consistently so that both the person completing the microcredential and anyone with whom the microcredential is shared has confidence that the completer has acquired the skill and transferred it into practice.

Self-Directed

When preparing to earn a microcredential, teachers consider the readiness of their students, their curriculum plan, the instructional approaches they are using in various lessons and units—even the school calendar. Applying a particular skill in context requires teachers to examine that context to determine when and in what way the microcredential task will best fit into their plans. Unlike a graduate course, there is no instructor, although in some cases teachers have access to formative feedback and other supports. Knowing what they will be expected to demonstrate, educators pursuing microcredentials must themselves make decisions about where they might have learning gaps and how to best fill those gaps. Unlike time-bound assignments—a paper with a due date, for example—high-quality microcredentials provide sufficient time for teachers to make intentional decisions about when and how to embed what they've learned in their work.

Accessible

The flexible timeline of microcredentials not only creates the opportunity for a more self-directed experience, but also makes the microcredential more accessible. Most of the microcredentials we know of are posted online and can be available almost anywhere. Fees for microcredentials vary widely and are generally dependent on the way in which the evidence is assessed. We believe that an indicator of quality is an external assessor who provides descriptive feedback and who is held accountable for assessing evidence reliably. This incurs a cost to the microcredential provider, which is typically passed on to the teacher, school, or district. Providers must attend to keeping costs as low as possible so that microcredentials are affordable.

Valid

Any educator who has designed a performance assessment knows that care must be taken to ensure alignment of the skill to be demonstrated, the criteria for assessing that skill, the task that learners will complete, and the evidence chosen from that task to be submitted for assessment. This match across all components of the microcredential ensures that the credential measures what it is supposed to measure. We encourage teachers to read the criteria and descriptors in their rubrics before beginning their work on the microcredential. These criteria and descriptors should give a clear picture of how the skill has been defined by the microcredential developers, as well as the level of rigor that will be expected when assessors review the evidence.

Using the information from this chapter, you should be able to "size up" a microcredential that you are considering using from two perspectives. First, does it match the definition of a microcredential? If so, it should be performance-based, focused on demonstration of a skill as applied in context, and able to be personalized. It should also incorporate such essential components as clear learning targets, success criteria, learning resources, a task, and a description of the evidence that will be used to assess competency. Second, does the microcredential reflect the additional quality criteria? If so, it will specify a standardized outcome while being self-directed, it will be accessible to users, and there will be strong alignment between the skill and the success criteria so that the credential is considered a valid measure of the skill.

In the next chapter, we'll look at how schools and districts might employ microcredentialing to build capacity and support organization-wide goals for student learning. We'll also begin to hear from the education agencies identified in the Introduction who are already using microcredentials. Their stories will help to illustrate the what, how, and why of microcredentials.

2

Meeting School and District Goals

In Albemarle, district leaders identified "significant disparities between racial groups in academic performance, achievement, and participation in academic programs" (Albemarle County Public Schools, 2021b). As a result, the district crafted an anti-racism policy that includes specific goals for equity. Among these goals are the following related to training educators within the district:

> All teachers and administrators shall be trained in cultural awareness and/or culturally responsive teaching practices. Culturally responsive teaching practices shall be incorporated into Board-approved appraisal systems, including the teacher appraisal system and the administrator performance appraisal. (Albemarle County Public Schools, 2021b)

A few years prior, the district had created several equity specialist positions, and those equity specialists began exploring the potential of using microcredentialing as one tool to help educators build proficiency in culturally responsive teaching and address district goals. After investigating several existing microcredentialing services, district leaders opted to create a homegrown credential that would be housed and evaluated within the district. As part of a larger state initiative, Albemarle also requires that all teachers and administrators complete some formal culturally responsive teaching training, either via microcredential or a more in-depth certification. As a result of these policies and incentives, they anticipate a continued increase in teachers and leaders completing the microcredential (Lars Holmstrom, personal communication, June 25, 2021).

As part of a grant, Winchester division leaders wanted to provide students in two elementary schools with an immersive experience in computer science and computational thinking by integrating it into the curriculum. Recognizing that many elementary teachers were hesitant about their own ability to provide meaningful instruction that integrated both curricular subject content and computer science skills, they chose to utilize microcredentials from two outside sources to provide this professional learning (Jennifer LaBombard-Daniels, personal communication, May 14, 2021).

Implementing a Centralized Approach to Microcredentials

Up to this point, our discussion has focused on the characteristics of high-quality microcredentials and their viability as a professional learning strategy. Practitioners pursuing individual opportunities for professional learning can apply the criteria outlined in Chapter 1 to evaluate and select existing credentials. When we first piloted our microcredentials, a call was sent out for educators who were interested in improving practices related to the larger topic of fostering a "learning-oriented classroom community." We offered a variety of credentials that aligned to this broader topic, such as "incorporating peer review and feedback" and "facilitating respectful student-to-student conversations." Educators were able to select from a menu of microcredentials based on their personal interests and goals. The educators completing these credentials found the work to be both personally and professionally rewarding as well as beneficial to student learning.

Our pilot was an example of a more decentralized approach to microcredentialing, one where individuals pursue and complete microcredentials without direct guidance from their school or district. In our work, we have found that this approach is effective for educators who are motivated to pursue specific goals, who may want to document skills in which they are already accomplished, or who enjoy learning on their own. In a few cases, we have seen teachers collaborate with colleagues to complete microcredentials, each of them doing their own work and providing their own evidence while comparing notes, asking each other questions, sharing resources, and giving each other feedback.

In this chapter, we describe how schools and districts might take a more centralized approach to microcredentialing through thoughtful planning and alignment to district and school goals. This type of approach, as described in the examples at the start of this chapter, focuses on how schools and districts might design or adopt a microcredentialing system so that all educators are "pulling in the same direction" to achieve a common goal or set of goals. Microcredentials are well suited to help schools and districts achieve short- and long-term goals because they are impact-oriented. They are designed for educators to apply complex, transferable skills and reflect on the impact of these changes in practice and on students. In addition, they can be used as part of a broader approach to professional learning—for example, as an accountability measure that complements other strategies (e.g., book studies, outside speakers, professional learning communities). As with any effective design, let's begin with the end in mind.

Planning Backward from Desired Outcomes

In their ubiquitous work on high-quality curriculum design, Wiggins and McTighe (2011) caution against the "twin sins" of planning and teaching. The first sin, *activity-oriented teaching,* occurs when educators plan activities focused primarily on student engagement and enjoyment at the expense of coherent and outcome-focused learning. Educators falling victim to this first sin tend to confuse "hands-on work with minds-on work" (p. 9). The second sin is *coverage-focused teaching,* which involves a steady march through a scope and sequence, pacing guide, textbook, or other resource. Teaching for "coverage" fails to prioritize the content, make it interesting for students, or provide students with opportunities for time and reflection to "uncover" ideas.

At some point during our time as students, we all have likely participated in learning that fell victim to these two sins. It is equally likely that we have also engaged in professional learning that was either activity-focused (e.g., an entertaining keynote speaker who shares a bevy of popular quotes) or coverage-focused (e.g., a one-day workshop to effectively differentiate your classroom). Like curriculum design, planning for high-quality, effective professional learning should begin with the end in mind by identifying specific outcomes and articulating their potential benefits to student learning. Approaching professional learning design this way can help to avoid these twin sins and provide a foundation for high-leverage, impactful experiences for teachers and leaders.

Guskey (2014) proposes a useful five-step approach for planning professional learning to avoid these twin sins. Following these steps can help schools and districts to clearly articulate desired outcomes and the processes needed to meet them:

1. **Articulate desired student learning outcomes.** Different sources of information can be used to identify areas of need, including large-scale and classroom assessments, classroom observations, attendance data, and so on. Information can be disaggregated to identify practices worth keeping and those in need of improvement.
2. **Identify how a change in practice will affect student learning.** The next step is to determine what practices, when implemented, might lead to the desired learning outcomes articulated in the first step. To do this, educators should seek out trustworthy research-based practices from peer-reviewed sources.
3. **Identify necessary organizational support(s) to implement these practices.** For this step, schools and districts must consider whether they have the needed resources (time, funding, support, etc.) to implement the practices outlined in step two. Also essential to step three is determining how feedback will be provided to help assess the impact of the new practices.
4. **Articulate desired educator knowledge and skills.** Step two suggests new practices that will benefit student learning, but it is in step four that specific knowledge and skills are articulated that provide tangible stepping-stones toward an overarching practice. When put together, these knowledge and skill goals result in changes in one or more practices. For example, a district looking to implement project-based learning (PBL) would need to focus on (1) creating driving questions to frame PBL, (2) providing scaffolded resources to support student learning, and (3) designing reliable and valid evaluation tools. Each of these skills supports the new practice being implemented.
5. **Evaluate and identify optimal professional learning activities.** There are many activities, coupled with organizational supports, in which educators can engage to develop the skills needed to implement new practices that will ultimately benefit student learning.

Microcredentials can be used either in isolation or as part of a broader professional learning initiative.

> ### From the Field: Planning Backward
>
> Although their process did not follow the exact order suggested by Guskey, Albemarle County Schools used district-level data to identify achievement, performance, and programmatic disparities between racial groups (step one) to determine that the educators were in need of training around equitable practices (step two). The district invested resources to promote this goal, including hiring equity specialists (step three) and identifying a set of specific outcomes in their anti-racism policy (step four). Finally, they explored options for professional learning, including microcredentials, that were focused on student learning outcomes and aligned with the articulated knowledge and skills (step five) (Lars Holmstrom, personal communication, June 25, 2021).
>
>
>
> In Los Angeles Unified, project-based learning (PBL) was the focus of implementation. Teachers and administrators from five alternative high schools were interested in focusing their curriculum on PBL to increase student engagement (step one) and decided to focus on PBL as a strategy to help teachers create authentic learning experiences that could increase student participation, attendance, and academic success (step two). The leadership team worked with Defined Learning, an existing district partner, to create a three-day learning experience supported by ongoing coaching and microcredentialing to help teachers implement PBL in their classrooms (step three). The microcredentials represent multiple domains of effective teaching and learning including planning, assessment, classroom environment, and leadership as they relate to PBL (step four). The specific tasks teachers completed to demonstrate their understanding directly related to their work in the classroom, allowing them to demonstrate transfer of learning from the traditional learning activities (in-person professional development, online modules, and coaching) to the successful completion of microcredentials

> as evidence of implementation (step five) (Simone Charles, personal communication, August 23, 2021).

To further illustrate this process, let's take a closer look at some additional scenarios where identifying school- or district-based needs, desired student learning outcomes, and associated changes in practices can lead to a needs-driven and research-based theory of action to support the use of microcredentials as a learning activity.

Crafting a Theory of Action

A theory of action, simply put, is an "if, then" statement that describes the relationship between specific actions and student learning outcomes. In our case, the "if" refers to the implementation of new practices, and the "then" identifies the desired impact on student learning. This theory should be grounded in research or theory *and* driven by school or district needs—both criteria are essential to a well-crafted, high-leverage theory of action. By analyzing teacher and student data, educators can develop a theory of action to articulate how an improvement in curriculum, assessment, instruction, or leadership should benefit students academically, social-emotionally, or both. Microcredentials, depending on their grain size, might be used in isolation or stacked with other similar credentials to help support the development of the skills outlined within a theory of action (more information on stacking microcredentials can be found in Chapter 3).

Below are three examples of theories of action that include school- or district-level data to support desired outcomes and references to research and theory supporting the benefit of these actions on student learning.

Example One

In a rural elementary school, learning walks consistently revealed that teachers weren't using ongoing assessment to determine the impact of their teaching on student learning. Testing data confirmed a large gap in student performance, particularly among students learning English. Based on this evidence, the school's principal decided that teachers needed to better understand why and how to use formative assessment in their classroom to create more responsive instruction. After reviewing research on this topic, she crafted the following theory of action to share with teachers:

> If teachers consistently monitor student progress using ongoing assessment, then they can better design instruction that is responsive to student needs. As a result, learning will be more visible to both the teachers and the students, boosting self-efficacy and student achievement (Hattie, 2012; Wiliam & Black, 1998).

The principal discussed this desired initiative with a colleague, who suggested that she explore a new stack of microcredentials called "Designing and Implementing Assessment *for* Learning" that was being offered through a state organization. Based on individual needs, teachers will be able to complete one or more of the credentials in this stack to improve their skills related to assessment and responsive instruction.

Example Two

At a large urban school district, leaders were concerned that the high school science curriculum offered wasn't preparing students to be "future ready" as outlined in their district mission statement. After hiring an outside organization to complete a curriculum audit, their concerns were confirmed. Specifically, one finding noted that "90 percent of the science curriculum materials within the district were at a level one or two on Webb's Depth of Knowledge (DOK) framework" (Webb, 2002). District leaders decided that curriculum designers needed support developing rigorous tasks that encourage more critical thinking, as well as training to implement those tasks. This theory of action followed:

> If curriculum is designed backward from authentic performance tasks, and teaching reflects the need to help students transfer their learning to new or unique situations, then student motivation and learning outcomes will improve, and [students] will be better prepared for the challenges of college and careers (Khattri et al., 1995; Krajcik et al., 2021; McTighe et al., 2020; Saavedra et al., 2021).

To address this theory, the district decided it would develop and offer a set of microcredentials around the broader topic of deeper learning to help increase rigor and relevance in classrooms. The "Deeper Learning" stack includes microcredentials on the following topics (selected depending on each learner's needs):

- Designing for deeper learning
- Creating student-friendly rubrics
- Differentiating for deeper learning
- Teaching for deeper learning

To implement this initiative, district leadership asked curriculum coaches to complete this Deeper Learning stack first so that they could then support and assess the teachers as they worked through them. To kick off teacher participation, the district brought in an outside presenter to provide a rationale for this work and review curriculum design software the district had purchased to house the assessments being developed. During the school year, teachers then completed the same microcredentials with support and feedback from curriculum coaches.

Example Three

A middle school principal received several emails from parents concerned that their children were being unreasonably punished for not turning in their algebra homework while learning remotely. These students were performing well on tests and quizzes but were struggling to stay motivated to complete day-to-day assignments, particularly when they already understood the content. The principal decided to review the grading practices of the four algebra teachers in her school and found that some combination of homework and classwork counted for 25 to 40 percent of students' grades in their classes. The message was clear: if students weren't consistently turning in homework, they had little chance at success. The principal decided that the school needed more consistent and equitable grading practices that focused on student learning versus compliance. However, for the school to improve its grading practices, she first needed to better understand how to lead them. Based on a review of grading research, she decided on the following theory of action to guide her own professional learning:

> If I help teachers implement more equitable grading practices within their classrooms, then grades will be increasingly free of bias and reflective of actual performance against standards, and students will be more motivated and in control of their learning (Feldman, 2018).

Next, the principal reached out to the professional learning coordinator for her district to see if any related microcredentials were offered. The learning coordinator suggested she complete a microcredential called "Avoiding Harmful Grading Practices" that was available through an outside organization. The job-embedded task associated with this microcredential involved randomly selecting 10 students within the school and recalculating their previous semester's grades using test, quiz, and performance assessment grades only, then developing a plan customized to support each teacher and context.

The results of the principal's analysis were startling—so much so, in fact, that she needed to be thoughtful about broaching this topic with her teachers. Counterproductive and harmful grading practices were so woven into the fabric of traditional report cards and grading that she needed to first help her teachers understand the impact these can have on students. She decided to have teachers review research on grading as part of their monthly professional learning community meetings before revising her theory of action for teachers and offering them the same microcredential to complete.

It is worth noting that theories of action are never truly "final." Along with the practices and student outcomes reflected within them, the theories should be refined from time to time based on a cycle of reflection and evaluation. This, of course, fits nicely with the use of microcredentialing as a pathway for participants to make positive progress toward identified targets and outcomes. Microcredentials are flexible in nature: as a theory of action evolves, school or district leadership can develop or seek out new credentials that align with a shift in direction or as the level of teaching and learning improves.

Creating Favorable Conditions for Learner Buy-In and Follow-Through

The success of any well-thought-out plan for professional learning, like those outlined above, is largely dependent on the degree to which learners are invested in changing their practices. We see the process of microcredential completion as a combination of (1) buying into a plan and (2) actually following through with the work and reflection needed to change practices and benefit student learning. Working against buy-in and follow-through in the pursuit of professional growth is the fact that educators often fail to recognize their potential to impact student learning. Research has found that teachers largely attribute the poor performance of their learners to *student* characteristics such as background or effort instead of to their own teaching—essentially shifting the responsibility for their struggles onto students (Evans et al., 2019). In actuality, evidence clearly shows that, among school-based factors, it is *teachers* who have the biggest impact on student performance (Hattie, 2009; Marzano, 2007). A perceived lack of control over student success, whether rooted in reality or not, can erode momentum from even the most well-intentioned initiatives. A second factor complicating the implementation of a well-thought-out professional learning plan is employment of a "one-size-fits-all" approach. All too often, educators complete prescribed activities to earn continuing education units (e.g., by attending a mandated workshop or symposium) without having any ownership over the direction of that learning or the outcomes associated with it.

Articulating a clear, research-based, and data-driven theory of action is the first important step in a professional learning plan. Equally essential is addressing impediments to success head-on by creating favorable conditions for professional learning. To do this, we suggest that professional learning plans include two other important elements: (1) opportunities for practice and feedback and (2) personalized pathways for growth.

Providing Opportunities for Practice and Feedback

The process of professional learning operates within a complex system (Reeves, 2010), and the challenge of creating favorable conditions for the buy-in and follow-through of educators engaged in learning is amplified when earning a microcredential is largely self-directed. If busy professionals are expected to invest the effort to master the skills these microcredentials are designed to develop, they must believe that those skills will transform their work with students. Among the most effective ways to establish this vital connection is through effective feedback on their completion of and reflection on the job-embedded tasks (Reeves, 2010). Just as incremental evidence of growth can help students establish a connection between effort and success, which leads to increased levels of motivation and perseverance (Stiggins, 2005), feedback can also support investment in the learning process for educators. Incremental feedback can help educators achieve "small successes" (Amabile & Kramer, 2011) to sustain them through the peaks and valleys of professional learning by understanding that progress, though messy at times, is being made. For microcredential tasks, this feedback can originate from three primary sources: (1) colleagues, school and district leaders, or outside evaluators tasked with scoring and awarding the credentials; (2) communities of practice or professional learning communities; and (3) action research on assessments that show an impact on student learning. One of the numerous benefits of using microcredentials is that they can be structured in such a way that feedback and support can come from any of these sources, and sometimes all three at once!

> **From the Field: Microcredential Feedback**
>
> At Albemarle, feedback comes from several sources. Practitioner work is initially evaluated by an assessment team that consists of individuals who have previously completed the culturally responsive teaching microcredential or certification. Teachers are also encouraged to meet monthly with their cohort to discuss their work and to informally provide each other with feedback. Finally, a primary focus of all required activities is to document impact on student learning, meaning teachers receive and review student data as feedback (Lars Holmstrom, personal communication, June 25, 2021).
>
>
>
> Winchester created the role of computer science integration coach for the two schools participating in the initiative to support teachers' completion of computer science microcredentials as they integrated this content more fully into their curriculum. Those in this role coach teachers to provide background knowledge, orient them as they begin the process, and help them collect evidence for the microcredentials (Amy Thomas, personal communication, May 25, 2021).
>
>
>
> Los Angeles Unified used professional development specialists from an outside organization who trained the teachers on how to review the completed microcredentials. The specialists developed rapport with teachers and were familiar with their work prior to providing detailed

> feedback on the artifacts submitted as part of the microcredentialing process (Simone Charles, personal communication, August 23, 2021).
>
>
>
> Richardson ISD uses staff from "expert departments" (such as coordinators and directors) as artifact reviewers because they have the expertise and passion as well as the breadth and depth of content knowledge to provide feedback. The expert reviewers also serve as coaches throughout the microcredentialing process. Teachers know to reach out to them when they need feedback or support prior to submission (Tabitha Branum, personal communication, May 21, 2021).

Let's briefly explore feedback for professional learning using one of the theories of action we previously introduced:

> If curriculum is designed backward from authentic performance tasks, and teaching reflects the need to help students transfer their learning to new or unique situations, then student motivation and learning outcomes will improve, and [students] will be better prepared for the challenges of college and careers (Khattri et al., 1995; Krajcik et al., 2021; McTighe et al., 2020; Saavedra et al., 2021).

Because the curriculum coaches detailed above had already completed their own stack of credentials on the design of these tasks, they each provided feedback to a cohort of several teachers. If any teachers struggled to submit their work within the two-month timeline set by the district, their assigned curriculum coach would follow up with them to determine what additional supports might be needed and establish a new timeline for completion. If submitted assignments and reflections did not meet mastery as outlined on the task rubrics, the curriculum coach would offer feedback so that teachers could revise and resubmit.

The district also set aside time each month for teachers to meet in school-level content-specific professional learning communities (PLCs). During the two months designated for the completion of these tasks, the PLC meetings were structured around the work being done to build the skill that the microcredential was designed to assess. Before beginning the microcredential, each PLC team was asked to select one resource from a list provided by the district that could serve as a common point of discussion for initial meetings. The group decided to investigate how Webb's DOK (Webb, 2002) could be used to plan increasingly rigorous activities for students. To complete the microcredential task, teachers were asked to design an activity or prompt for students at level three or four of Webb's DOK framework. Individually, teachers planned a task or prompt aligned with these levels and used it with their students. They then met in their PLCs to analyze and discuss student work and what changes might be needed to better meet the goal of preparing students to transfer their learning. After these collective discussions, each PLC member completed the remaining microcredential reflection. At the next PLC meeting, the group revised their professional learning goals based on the impact their work has had on students. Through this process, teachers were able to receive feedback from both colleagues (within their PLCs) and student work (which was examined as one of the PLC protocols).

Personalizing Professional Learning

One of the points we make throughout this book is that microcredentials offer a personalized approach to professional learning. We've already discussed how microcredentials are both personalized and self-directed, in large part based on the situational context for each individual learner (e.g., grade level or subject) and the resources that they can access when completing a microcredential. Here, we explore yet another path for personalizing microcredentials within a larger theory of action: providing choice. To explore how to offer learners choice and flexibility while still addressing the goals identified within a theory of action, let's revisit another of our sample theories of action:

> If teachers consistently identify learning goals and monitor student progress toward these goals, then learning will be more visible to both the teachers and the students themselves, boosting self-efficacy and achievement (Hattie, 2012; Wiliam & Black, 1998).

To help teachers address this goal, they are asked to develop competency in the following building-block skills, each with its own aligned microcredential:

1. Unpack standards to identify specific learning goals that will help me align and target instructional activities so that students better understand what they are learning and why they are learning it.
2. Align formative, ongoing assessments to learning goals that will help students become more reflective and autonomous learners.
3. Analyze formative assessments to identify patterns in student learning and use that information to design responsive instruction that scaffolds students as they work to meet a particular learning objective.
4. Provide effective feedback to students, which will help students know the processes and self-regulation needed to improve their learning.

Based on feedback from walkthroughs, one group of 4th grade teachers decided that they would like to start with the first of these building-block skills and associated microcredential—unpacking standards to identify specific learning goals. Meanwhile, a 2nd grade team that had attended a conference session earlier in the year on using assessment evidence to drive instructional design opted for the third building-block goal and microcredential (analyzing formative assessments to identify patterns in student learning and using that information to design responsive instruction). The principal encouraged teachers to "stack" more than one credential if they were ready to develop additional skills. Teachers could complete any number of microcredentials within the stack depending on their professional growth needs and interests. As a result, professional learning was tailored to the needs of the school as well as the needs of individual teachers.

A rich, well-crafted theory such as this one provides several potential entry points and pathways for teachers to pursue the larger goal of making learning visible through ongoing assessment, feedback, and adjustment. Teachers can identify these personalized entry points and pathways through classroom walkthroughs or PLC discussions, or they can select them based on personal interest.

From the Field: Personalized Pathways

At Albemarle, teachers completing the culturally responsive teaching microcredential can choose specific areas of focus for their work within a larger culturally responsive teaching framework. At the top level, practitioners can select to work on "cultural lenses, curriculum and instruction, or partnerships." Within each of these broader categories are indicators and sub-indicators that specify look-fors, or specific competencies, to demonstrate when completing the microcredential. After selecting a culturally responsive teaching category, practitioners then select several sub-indicators as the specific areas of focus for their work. For example, within the larger category of curriculum and instruction, a participant might choose to focus on "lesson planning that embraces student differences" or "incorporating frequent checks for understanding to promote growth among all learners." Layering choice this way allows educators to pursue areas of interest or of relevance to their unique situation (e.g., content area or grade level) (Lars Holmstrom, personal communication, June 25, 2021).

Richardson ISD acknowledges that educators are professionals who know their strengths, opportunities, and the students they teach. By giving the practitioners the choice of not only how many microcredentials to complete, but also topic and length of time, they are able to decide what best meets their needs and what they want to improve. Rubrics are customized for each artifact, and choice is offered within each microcredential. Part of the process includes supporting practitioners as they determine what evidence best shows what they have learned (Tabitha Branum, personal communication, May 21, 2021).

The best professional learning experiences are rooted in clear goals and align with research-based practices intended to improve student outcomes. Microcredentials are also largely self-directed, which increases the need for self-motivation and investment on the part of the learner. To create favorable conditions for learner buy-in and follow-through, professional learning plans using microcredentials should include well-crafted theories of action, opportunities for educators to receive feedback from various sources, and pathways for personal growth. We have more to say about the nuts and bolts of implementing microcredentials in Chapter 5 and the role of leadership in Chapter 6.

In the next two chapters, we look more closely at the tools and strategies needed to adopt or design microcredentials to assist educators in developing the skills needed—whether the decision to complete them originates from an individual (decentralized) or from the school or district (centralized).

3

Selecting Microcredentials

When Winchester Public Schools in Virginia received a USDOE Education Innovation and Research Early-Phase Grant to support the integration of computer science and computational thinking into their curriculum, they knew their teachers would need high-quality learning experiences to support these innovative computer science instructional practices. Due to the range of background knowledge and skills possessed by their educators, the district determined that microcredentials provided the best pathway to more personalized professional learning. In researching the competencies that were necessary, the division found existing microcredentials that met their needs. In this case, the choice was made to go with these outside microcredentials rather than create them internally (Jennifer LaBombard-Daniels, personal communication, May 14, 2021).

Richardson ISD began their microcredential development by identifying desired outcomes based on broad goals of what "master teachers" would know, understand, and be able to do in a classroom. District leaders and select teachers worked together to create a list of possible microcredential topics such as social-emotional learning and cultural competency. Professional learning teams hosted by departments with expertise in these topics developed lists of desired outcomes for microcredentials. For example, representatives from the counseling department developed criteria for social-emotional learning while representatives from the diversity, equity, and inclusion department created the criteria for cultural competence. Each team worked to answer questions like "What does this topic/term really mean?" "What does competency in this skill look like in a classroom?" and "How can we shift this learning from a traditional workshop format to a microcredential?" Once these key decisions were made, the teams examined resources available from vendors with whom they had existing relationships that were offering microcredentials, using their shared understanding to customize already-written microcredentials to the local context. In cases where existing microcredentials were not readily available, teams worked to design microcredentials locally (Tabitha Branum, personal communication, May 21, 2021).

As these examples show, microcredentials are available from a variety of sources, sometimes at no cost. Why, then, would school districts invest resources in designing their own microcredentials? The "adopt or design" decision requires time and exploration at the outset of any microcredentialing initiative.

School districts have a variety of challenges and needs, and not all situations are like those in Winchester or Richardson. Done well, district- or school-designed microcredentials that reflect the quality criteria outlined in this book require training, collaboration, time, and resources that not all school districts have available. At the same time, microcredentials acquired from outside sources that don't target specific needs or goals, are more compliance-oriented than competency-based, or are unlikely to affect student learning can become "just another thing to check off" rather than a meaningful, beneficial learning experience.

Ultimately, the decision to adopt or design microcredentials must be made carefully, based on the unique situation of each school or district. Key questions to consider when deciding to adopt or design include the following:

1. Are there existing credentials that align with district or school goals? Before engaging in the design process, we recommend reviewing available microcredentials using a checklist like the one in Figure 3.1 to check each one against the key traits outlined in Chapter 1. (See Appendix A for a blank version of the checklist.) It is important to go beyond the title of the microcredential to assess its quality, including by checking to see that learning goals, success criteria, activities, and content are all aligned to one another. Diving into the details of the microcredential prior to adoption can also indicate how well the microcredential matches the district's or school's professional learning focus. Three different microcredentials focusing on differentiating instruction, for example, may take three very different approaches to this skill or even define the skill in three different ways.

FIGURE 3.1
Microcredential Key Traits Checklist Example

Key Traits	Evidence for Adoption
Performance-Based • A microcredential reflects transfer of learning or application of skills in authentic and complex situations. One or more skill-based objectives are included that align with the rigor of the performance-based task(s). • Successful completion of the microcredential is based on evidence that the learner is proficient in the skill. Credentials are not awarded simply based on a time requirement.	✓ The microcredential asks practitioners to complete a unit plan that includes standards-aligned learning goals, key assessments, and learning events to help students master these learning goals and prepare them for the designed assessments. To earn the microcredential, submissions must meet quality criteria that demonstrate proficiency.
Contextual • Completion of the microcredential is based on evidence that a skill has been applied in the context of the learner's work. • Learners engage in active reflection on how the skills being applied influence their daily practices and ultimately their students.	✓ The unit plans were specific to the content and grade level of each practitioner. X There is no specific requirement for submissions to include teacher reflection. Can we address this through team and PLC meeting agendas?
Personalized • Responses to the prompt or task will be unique to each learner, reflecting the learner's context, background knowledge, and application of the skill(s). • A variety of resources is provided for learners, which may include open access readings (book chapters, articles, blog posts), videos, podcasts, websites, and so on. Some "challenge" resources are included for learners with higher levels of readiness.	✓ Individual teachers will design or select their own lessons/learning experiences and assessments. X The microcredential itself does not provide resources. Perhaps we should provide some sample units and resources on alignment.

continued

FIGURE 3.1 *continued*
Microcredential Key Traits Checklist Example

Key Traits	Evidence for Adoption
Standardized • Although responses to learning experiences will vary depending on the learner, the microcredential provides clear expectations and guidance for the completion of tasks to limit variations in quality. • Assessors will be or have been trained in consistent and reliable scoring of microcredential submissions.	✓ To receive the credential, all units must adhere to the specified set of design criteria outlined in the rubric. ✓ The microcredential provider provides external assessment for a fee. We need to be sure to budget for this.
Self-Directed • The learner selects and accesses resources and opportunities that will be helpful in preparing to meet the requirements of the task. • The learner determines the timing and scheduling for any job-embedded tasks, including the length of time needed to design and implement the task requirements (e.g., spacing out the teaching of two lessons to provide adequate time for reflection and revision). • Individual learners decide where in the curriculum or in the context of their work the skill is best applied so that the task can be completed in the most authentic, job-embedded way possible.	✓ Practitioners are given the first semester to select a window of content to design and implement a unit of study.
Accessible • The microcredential is easily available and affordable. • The microcredential has a flexible completion timeline to adapt to the needs and resources of adult learners. • The microcredential is readily accessed. Evidence and feedback can be easily submitted and viewed regardless of the platform or learning management system used.	✓ The assessment fee is the only cost. We can budget to cover this for all teachers over two semesters. ✓ A semester-long timeline should be more than sufficient. School leaders will periodically check in with participants to ensure that they are making progress on the task. ✓ Evidence is submitted online, and assessors have the option of providing annotated feedback that can be easily viewed by the educator completing the microcredential.

Valid	
• The evidence to be submitted, the resources provided, and the descriptors in the microcredential rubric clearly align with the identified skill(s). • It is possible to derive the microcredential's skill(s) by reviewing the rubric criteria and descriptors. The level of rigor of the task aligns with the skill(s). • Evaluative criteria are specific and detailed enough for consistent scoring across submissions.	✓ The microcredential has a clear objective—teachers develop a unit plan with standards-aligned learning goals, assessments to measure those goals, and learning events to equip students with the skills and knowledge measured by those assessments. To determine the degree to which the microcredential measures this objective, the district leadership team examined the alignment to the learning objective, task, and rubric and agreed that, based on the information available, the microcredential was both valid and reliable.

2. Will teachers have a variety of microcredentials to choose from, or will credentials be chosen centrally to align to district or school needs? If teachers have autonomy to pursue options of individual interest or need, then adopting a suite of microcredentials could accommodate a range of potential topics. Alternatively, one or more microcredentials could be adopted that align with a priority such as cultural competence, formative assessment, or project-based learning. This more focused approach limits educators' ability to choose their own learning goals but is justified in situations where building capacity in a specific area is important to meeting district or school goals. In these cases, we encourage adopters of microcredentials to carefully consider the degree of personalization reflected in each microcredential to ensure that educators still have opportunities to personalize their learning.

The most direct way to guarantee that microcredentials will meet district or school goals, of course, is for the district or school to design them. The design process, which we will describe in detail in the next chapter, can be labor-intensive and requires both training and resources. Still, it has advantages that can make it worthwhile. In some school districts, like Albemarle County, it is itself a meaningful learning experience for designers and results in microcredentials that are uniquely suited to the needs of existing staff as well as specifically matched to local goals.

3. If microcredentials from outside sources are being considered, have they been vetted by internal or external reviewers? Providers of microcredentials should offer information about how and by whom their microcredentials were designed and reviewed.

In our own design process, we conduct two rounds of reviews. An author's draft is first reviewed by another microcredential designer from our team who is asked to assess specific design features, including the key traits from Chapter 1. After a first revision, we seek reviews from practitioners who provide valuable feedback from the perspective of users. Regardless of the specifics, information about design and review should be readily available and should convince potential adopters that the microcredential was designed according to a rigorous process that included review, feedback, and revision.

4. How does the school or district anticipate using microcredentials in the future? If microcredentialing is used infrequently to advance the skills of professional staff (e.g., to achieve consistent implementation of a specific instructional initiative), it may be more efficient to adopt existing microcredentials if they are available. By contrast, in cases where a school or district intends to commit to an emphasis on competency-based professional learning, making it a lasting component of the culture, it may be worth investing in training and support for internal microcredential design. Once a process is in place for design and review of microcredentials, it can be refined and replicated over time to meet the changing learning needs of educators.

> ### From the Field: Aligning Microcredentials with School Goals and Educator Interests
>
> Los Angeles Unified selected a series of microcredentials to meet their goal of building teacher and leader capacity to implement high-quality project-based learning. They selected nine microcredentials organized in categories such as instruction, assessment, classroom environment, and leadership. Originally, they intended to have all participants complete the same microcredentials, but as teams of teachers worked together and learned more about project-based learning, some adjustments were made to the original sequence. All participants were still asked to complete nine microcredentials from the same categories, but educators were able to personalize the experience as their interests and needs evolved over time by selecting from a larger catalog of options with similar learning outcomes.

Using Key Traits as Criteria When Adopting Microcredentials

Microcredentials are available from numerous sources and reflect varying degrees of quality. It is likely that teachers, schools, or districts interested in microcredentials will easily find ones related to particular areas of interest. In such cases, the credentials can be evaluated against key traits and variables in a checklist like the one in Figure 3.1.

To illustrate how the checklist might be used to evaluate existing microcredentials, consider the example of a small school district that lacks a guaranteed and viable curriculum. This district has three elementary schools, two middle schools, and one high school. District and school leaders have consistently documented a piecemeal approach to curriculum design in which teachers regularly scour the internet for materials that might help them teach state standards. The director of curriculum and instruction determined that teachers needed support in curriculum design so that they could begin the process of developing a more comprehensive curriculum including a scope and sequence, available resources, and assessments. Although the district will hire teachers to work over the summer to develop this curriculum, administrators also recognize that all faculty need professional learning around curriculum and assessment design. After reviewing a variety of options, they selected the following microcredential by checking it against the key traits in Figure 3.1:

- **Title:** Standards-Aligned Unit Design
- **Learning target:** Create learning experiences and assessments that align with discrete learning goals derived from standards.
- **Task:** Teachers complete a unit plan that includes standards-aligned learning goals, key assessments, and learning events to help students master the learning goals and prepare them for the designed assessments. Teachers submit the standards, learning goals, at least one formative assessment, the summative assessment, and lesson plans for three learning experiences from their units.
- **Reflection:** Before completing the task, teachers reflect on how they identify the content to be taught during each lesson or unit, as well as on their process for creating assessments. After completing the task, they reflect on how this increased focus on alignment affected student clarity about learning expectations and unit/lesson performance.

- **Learning resources:** A video on unpacking standards to identify learning goals and an article on standards-aligned assessment design.
- **The rubric:** Success criteria in the rubric include not only the presence of the required submissions from teachers, but also the features of those submissions that provided evidence of alignment with standards. There are also rubric criteria that align specifically with the pre- and post-reflections that teachers are asked to submit.

Variables Among High-Quality Microcredentials

In addition to ensuring that microcredentials reflect key traits, adopters should also consider the following variables to determine if they meet individual needs.

Grain Size

The "micro" part of microcredential suggests that to successfully complete the task, a teacher would need to demonstrate a narrowly defined skill. But what do we mean by "narrow?" How broad or comprehensive can a skill be and still be "micro?" Developers have a range of answers to these questions, as evidenced by the variety of microcredentials available—everything from completion of a credential in an afternoon to a series of activities more indicative of the work involved in a college course. Finding the right grain size isn't an exact science, but it does take careful reflection on the part of the adopter (or designer). Microcredentials are intended to be completed as part of the daily activities that take place in classrooms and schools. When the work extends too far beyond this realm, then the grain size becomes too large. To test if a microcredential has an appropriate grain size, we suggest considering the following three questions:

1. **Is the microcredential doable for most educators?** Consideration should be given to educators' capacity to devote the time and energy necessary to master the learning target and successfully complete the aligned learning task and reflections.
2. **Can evidence be collected within the scope of a few activities (though they may be distributed over time) that document the learning target?** The target and the success criteria should be narrow enough that they can be observed within the scope of one or a

few activities. (Although an activity is often a lesson, it could also be another type of interaction, such as a conference with a parent or student, a coaching session, or a team meeting.)

3. **Can the evidence required for documentation be evaluated by an external assessor in one sitting?** Success criteria should be evident in the documentation that educators submit to earn the microcredential. If the assessor needs to review an entire portfolio or more than a handful of artifacts, then the grain size may be too large.

If the answer to the above questions is yes, then the microcredential is likely of a reasonable grain size. (See Chapter 4 for further detail and examples of how to design learning targets.)

Stacks

Stacking is a strategy for keeping each microcredential at a reasonable grain size while providing a path to a deeper or broader skill set. For example, the National Education Association (2021) offers a microcredential stack in classroom management that includes the following six separate microcredentials:

1. Addressing Challenging Behaviors
2. Aspects of an Engaged Classroom
3. Classroom Expectations and Routines
4. Creating a Classroom Community
5. Organizing the Physical Layout of the Classroom
6. Trauma-Informed Pedagogy

Classroom management skills are multifaceted and include multiple areas of competency, so the grain size is much too broad for a single microcredential. This stack provides microcredentials of more appropriate grain size, enabling educators to choose targeted classroom management skills according to their learning needs. Some educators might earn multiple microcredentials from the stack, enabling them to build broad expertise in classroom management while focusing on one competency at a time.

A microcredential stack may have no particular sequence, but sometimes there is a suggested progression, as in this stack from VASCD:

1. Modeling Empathy
2. Teaching Students About Empathy
3. Creating Opportunities for Students to Cultivate Empathy

The order of this stack suggests that modeling empathy is foundational to teaching students about empathy, and that students need to understand something about empathy before being able to demonstrate it in their own interactions. Although a learning path is suggested here, learners are still free to choose any one of these three microcredentials as a starting point.

Support/Guidance

It is generally expected that educators will complete the requirements for their microcredentials independently, receiving feedback on their submissions but not direct instruction. Opportunities for educators to access guidance and support as they are working toward a microcredential vary among different designs. One common practice is for one or more points in the process—following the pre-reflection, for example—to be identified at which teachers are given feedback on the work they've submitted so far. We support this type of formative assessment, which can reassure educators they are on the right track, point out an aspect of their work that they might want to build upon, or note a misperception that suggests a need to revisit learning resources before undertaking the performance task. At the same time, to protect the self-directed nature of the microcredential, this feedback should be descriptive rather than corrective, and it should be left to the educator to determine whether and how to use the feedback in completing the microcredential.

Teachers who are unfamiliar with microcredentials may expect something similar to a minicourse or a class, with an expectation that there will be an instructor explaining, directing, providing guidance, and coaching them throughout. Though guided instruction through a set of instructional modules may provide a valuable learning experience for educators, we would not classify this model as a microcredential.

Our microcredential design invites educators to seek guidance and support from sources within their learning environment if they believe it would be helpful. For example, a teacher working on a microcredential might share his work with a coach or teammate and ask for feedback, observe a colleague he believes has mastered the skill he is developing, or even attend a related workshop or webinar. But these opportunities for guidance are not typically built into the microcredential; rather, they are choices that educators make as professionals determining their own learning needs.

Before educators adopt a microcredential for use within a school or district, we recommend reviewing all available information regarding any support or feedback that will be available from the provider. Additionally, it is important to be clear about how much latitude educators will have to seek out guidance on their own as they are working to earn the microcredential.

Learning Resources

As we've previously noted, we see microcredentials as modeling both assessment *for* learning and assessment *of* learning. We believe that the process of earning the microcredential helps educators both to demonstrate a skill and to strengthen it. In our model, the teacher chooses any learning resources. We believe that personalization and choice are key elements of a high-quality microcredential, and we believe in the ability of teachers to choose the resources that best meet their learning needs. Though we might occasionally include recommended readings in a microcredential, this would only be the case if those readings were essential to the teacher's success (e.g., a glossary of key terms).

Consider, for example, VASCD's "Creating a Performance Assessment Blueprint" microcredential. This microcredential is part of a stack related to performance assessment that also includes microcredentials on designing tasks, developing rubrics, and scaffolding student learning. The blueprint microcredential requires teachers to formulate a learning goal that they believe is best assessed using a performance-based task and a rubric, then create the skeleton of a plan that shows how the various components of the performance assessment align with one another and with the learning goal. This microcredential offers a list of about a dozen optional learning resources as well as one recommended resource—a blog post titled "What Is Performance Assessment?" by Tom VanderArk (2013) available at www.gettingsmart.com/2013/12/26/performance-assessment/. We selected this blog post as a recommended resource because it is a single short document that addresses the essential aspects of performance assessment. Our view is that even educators who have expertise in this area and use performance assessment regularly should have these essentials in mind as they approach the microcredential task. For the most part, however, we keep recommended resources to a minimum when designing microcredentials. Instead, we attempt to provide a variety of resources so that teachers can select those that best fit their needs. We remind ourselves that the purpose of learning resources is to help the teacher prepare to be successful on the task.

In some instances, microcredentials are built around sequenced sets of resources that define a required learning path. Though this alone does not preclude a microcredential from being high in quality, these learning resources should be foundational and connected to the task that educators will complete. When considering microcredentials for possible adoption, we suggest that reviewers pay careful attention to the accompanying learning resources. They should be sufficient in both number and variety to meet most educators' needs. They should be easily accessible and updated periodically (especially if they are accessed online). Most important, they should clearly support the learning targets so that educators who use them will find them useful and relevant to their work completing the microcredential.

Assessment and Timing of Feedback

Adopters should ensure not only that a microcredential meets the indicators for quality, but also that the evidence will be assessed in a way that inspires confidence in the outcome. Before they begin, they should understand who will be assessing their work and what that assessment will look like.

As an example, members of a grade-level team might all work toward a microcredential together, giving and receiving feedback as they complete the work. Then the team may sit down with all the evidence to discuss strengths, ongoing learning needs, and goals. In other cases, external validation that educators have met success criteria may be important, such as when a microcredential is used to gain relicensure or as part of an application for a leadership role. In cases where external assessment is planned, assessors should receive training and engage in protocols to ensure an appropriate level of reliability. Information about this aspect of microcredential assessment should be available to potential adopters, who will have their own school's or district's purpose in mind and therefore be able to match assessment plans to it.

It is also important to consider when in the process feedback will be given. Is it important that teachers receive feedback along the way, or only at the end, when all work has been submitted? If the success criteria are not met, does the teacher have the option to resubmit evidence? Again, these decisions relate to purpose. As we noted earlier, formative feedback might be available from a variety of school-based sources as well as from the microcredential provider. If the microcredential evidence will be used to award continuing education credits, credit toward an endorsement, or a digital badge, then minimal, standardized formative feedback may be preferred.

We have discussed how key traits (criteria) and variables can be applied to the adoption of high-quality microcredentials. In the next chapter, we take a closer look at the microcredential design process.

4

Designing Microcredentials

The microcredentials being used in Utah were developed by a variety of individuals and groups, including institutions of higher education, school districts, charters, and regional service centers, among others. With several different individuals and groups involved in the design process, there is a variety of evidence that educators completing the microcredentials can submit, ranging from lesson plans to videos to student work. However, a nonnegotiable element of these designs, regardless of the format of the evidence collected, is that educators should document both *competence* and *consistency* of the identified skills and learning targets. As a result, the Utah State Board of Education (USBE) provides assistance in preparing the microcredentials using their online platform, MIDAS, to ensure that the alignment between the tasks and the outcomes—as well as the degree to which they are integrated into classroom practice—are integral to their offerings (Daron Kennett, personal communication, August 12, 2021).

As the USBE example illustrates, it is important that designers are thoughtful regarding the appropriate key traits and variables described in Chapter 3. In this chapter, we describe each essential component in detail along with the key traits and variables that are most important for designers to consider.

Skills

Microcredentials are intended to certify proficiency in one or more skills that should be clear, competency-based, and can be measured using evidence from authentic tasks. These skills should be articulated using action verbs and in measurable terms and should clearly describe what the learner who earns the microcredential is able to do. Because the microcredential tasks and reflections should encourage educators to apply their learning to unique situations or contexts, it is essential that all skills reflect this expectation for learning transfer. A skill such as "remember the elements of building classroom community" does not ask an educator to do anything with that learning beyond remembering it. For true transfer of learning, the skill might instead state "develop a comprehensive approach to building classroom community and relationships with students." Readers familiar with Bloom's taxonomy (Anderson & Krathwohl, 2001) or Webb's Depth of Knowledge (Webb, 2002) might recognize that these skills generally align with Bloom's Analyze, Evaluate, or Create levels or Webb's levels three or four. Some possible verbs that designers could use to generate these skills include *design, compare and contrast, judge, develop, appraise, construct, plan, generate, revise, assess,* and *investigate*.

A second key consideration in designing skills is the issue of grain size. In Chapter 3, we suggested three questions that are helpful for determining whether the grain size is appropriate when adopting existing microcredentials. In this chapter, when considering the design of skills and settling on the appropriate grain size, we invoke a common fairy tale.

Consider grain size in the context of the Goldilocks story. If the skill is too narrow and can be demonstrated by most people without much effort, it may not be worthy of a microcredential (e.g., unpacking a standard to identify key vocabulary students need to learn). If the skill is too broad, the success criteria are likely to be numerous or vague and the evidence cumbersome and difficult to assess reliably (e.g., creating an entire scope and sequence for 7th grade social studies). When the skill is more comprehensive, we suggest breaking it into smaller components and creating a collection or "stack" of microcredentials. Even when the skill is "just right" in terms of grain size, it can still be helpful to list any subskills (which are referred to in this book as learning targets) that will be embedded in the microcredential so that the steps necessary to demonstrate the skill are clear to learners from the outset. (See Figure 4.1 for examples of skills that are too small, too big, and just right.)

The following example shows how learning targets can indicate how the skill is being defined and how it will be demonstrated.

FIGURE 4.1
Skills: Too Small, Too Big, and Just Right

Too Small	Just Right	Too Big
Develop a set of sentence starters to guide student-to-student feedback.	Select, implement, and evaluate structured protocols for student-to-student feedback.	Plan for and conduct instructional rounds to assess the use of student-to-student feedback within the school.
Curate a set of icebreaker activities.	Encourage respectful classroom dialogue through modeling and guided practice.	Analyze and evaluate the literature related to respectful classroom dialogue and create a resource for other teachers.
Plan instructional questions that encourage inquiry.	Design an instructional unit that combines content acquisition and deeper learning goals.	Rewrite a curriculum to better reflect a balanced instructional approach that includes both surface-level goals and goals for deeper learning.

Skill: Create and effectively communicate clear learning goals.
Learning targets:
- Create "lesson-sized" learning goals aligned to standards.
- Express learning targets in student-friendly language.
- Engage students in activities designed to help them understand learning goals.
- Informally assess student understanding of the learning goals.

A teacher considering this microcredential can easily imagine what the task to be completed and the evidence to be submitted might look like.

When developing skills and learning targets, consider the key traits *performance-based* **and** *standardized* **and the variables** *grain size* **and** *stacking*. **Ensure that they are aligned with the other three components.**

Success Criteria

Success criteria for microcredentials clearly define the broader skill and describe how evidence of competence will be assessed. These criteria usually appear in a rubric. We encourage designers to keep their focus on qualitative aspects of the evidence rather than mere compliance by completing activities.

For instance, consider this skill from the example earlier: "Create and effectively communicate clear learning goals." A criterion for compliance might be "Teacher has submitted a list of learning goals." This allows the teacher and assessor to check a box, but it does not describe a level of competence in the skill. Instead, we would recommend describing features of qualities of the evidence that indicate competence, such as the following: "The learning goals submitted by the teacher are written in student-friendly language such that learners would be able to clearly explain what they are learning if prompted by the teacher or an outside observer."

There are three types of rubrics for use with microcredentials:

- **Analytic rubrics** provide an opportunity for assessors to break down a task into its component parts, or traits, alerting microcredential participants to areas where they have shown clear understanding or misconceptions.
- **Holistic rubrics** show teachers how the combination of skills they are working on merge into a cohesive whole, meaning that all the traits are described together versus separately in the analytic rubric.
- **Single-point rubrics** (also known as **criterion performance lists**) are increasingly popular and provide a simple method for assessors to determine whether teachers have met expectations, with space for descriptive feedback. Unlike analytic and holistic rubrics, they lack descriptors of different levels of performance. However, by providing space for descriptive feedback, this kind of rubric creates a clear, seamless pathway for resubmission if that is part of the assessment process.

Regardless of the rubric's format, it is essential that it provide clear, unambiguous success criteria. These criteria must be written at a level of detail that both helps to guide learners and allows assessors to use them reliably. The Council of Chief State School Officers (2020) offers assessment principles for microcredentials that include "tailored assessment," meaning that "rubrics should be tailored to align with the specific competency, not based on a generic rubric" (p. 3). We would add that microcredential rubrics can be targeted even further by referencing task-specific indicators that show evidence of the competency being assessed.

Figure 4.2 shows how rubric criteria can be derived from learning targets. It is essential that the descriptors accurately reflect the intentions of the identified targets. Figure 4.3 shows a completed rubric including the aligned learning targets.

When developing success criteria, consider the key traits *performance-based, standardized,* and *valid* and the variables *assessment* and *feedback*. Ensure that they are aligned with the other three components.

FIGURE 4.2
Rubric Criteria Derived from Learning Targets

Learning Target	Rubric Criteria and Descriptor
Provide students with the tools and modeling necessary to reflect on their strengths and needs as learners.	Students' reflections of their strengths and needs as learners are descriptive enough to paint a detailed picture of their self-awareness as learners.
Apply community-building strategies to help learners feel safe, valued, and confident.	Evidence shows examples of students interacting with a variety of peers in respectful, supportive ways. Students are comfortable sharing their beliefs, values, and needs with one another.
Build students' questioning skills in order to enhance their abilities to think at higher cognitive levels.	Evidence includes student-generated questions that demonstrate higher-level thinking about the skill or content as outlined by one or more questioning framework (e.g., Gallagher and Ascher's [1963] questioning taxonomy).

FIGURE 4.3
Sample Rubric for Driving Questions Microcredentials

The single-point rubric below lists success criteria for the skill of creating and using driving questions to prompt deeper learning. The learning targets are as follows:

- Expand students' understanding of how driving questions can lead to deeper learning.
- Use driving questions to engage students in inquiry-based learning through discussion, dialogue, and/or research.
- Reflect on the impact of driving questions on student engagement and learning.

The microcredential task has three parts: a pre-reflection, an activity, and a post-reflection. The activity asks teachers to design a unit or a series of learning experiences around a driving question with aligned learning standards/objectives. Students respond to the question before and after the unit or series of lessons. The teacher observes student engagement and examines student work to reflect on the effect of planning around the driving question.

Single-Point Rubric for Pre-Reflection, Activity, and Post-Reflection

Task	Success Criteria	Assessor Feedback
Pre-reflection	Response fully addresses the pre-reflection prompt with enough detail for the reader to know the teacher's current understanding of the use of driving questions to drive student inquiry and/or progress toward deeper learning goals. Responses to the pre-reflection questions provide context for the teacher's classroom environment.	
Activity: Planning	Questions are chosen that are engaging, open-ended, and aligned with learning goals for students. The evidence submitted clearly documents how these questions will be implemented within the planned learning experiences.	
Activity: Student work	Artifacts (written or video) from learning activities demonstrate that interaction with driving questions led to student engagement and deeper learning (i.e., higher-level cognitive skills are demonstrated).	

Post-reflection	Response demonstrates careful observation and analysis of student interaction and work and draws conclusions that are supported by the evidence submitted for the task.	

Resources

Articles, book chapters, websites, podcasts, videos, expert and practitioner blogs, and so on are integral to microcredentials. These resources help educators better understand both the importance of completing a given microcredential and also specific next steps they might take to improve their practices. We encourage designers to select resources in more than one media format. We also recommend that designers include extension resources for those who might be looking to take their learning to the next level.

As an example, here is the list of resources available for our microcredential "Creating a Performance Assessment Blueprint."

Resources: These learning resources are provided to help participants prepare to complete the task. Learners should select those that are most helpful to them and consider accessing other resources and learning opportunities. Participants need not use all resources unless they choose to do so.

Recommended resource:

- For a quick overview of performance assessment, it is recommended that participants first read "What Is Performance Assessment?" by Tom VanderArk (www.gettingsmart.com/2013/12/26/performance-assessment/).

Optional resources:

- A simplified example of planning a performance assessment is discussed in "Performance-Based Assessment: Reviewing the Basics" by Patricia Hilliard (www.edutopia.org/blog/performance-based-assessment-reviewing-basics-patricia-hilliard).
- National standards in the content areas are often good sources of transferable learning goals. These are just examples; consult the national standards for your content area:

- Next Generation Science Standards (www.nextgenscience.org/)
        - Standards for the English Language Arts (https://ncte.org/resources/standards/ncte-ira-standards-for-the-english-language-arts/)
        - National Core Arts Standards (www.nationalartsstandards.org/)
- Resources related to big ideas, questions, or problems:
    - "Structuring the Curriculum Around Big Ideas" by Janet Alleman, Barbara Knighton, and Jere Brophy (www.socialstudies.org/system/files/publications/articles/yl_230225.pdf)
    - PBLWorks projects that begin with driving questions (https://my.pblworks.org/projects)
- Resources related to tasks:
    - "Designing Performance Assessment Tasks" by Philip N. Cohen (www.ascd.org/el/articles/designing-performance-assessment-tasks)
    - Samples of student projects (tasks) from High Tech High (www.hightechhigh.org/student-work/projects/)
    - "Framework of Assessment Approaches" by Jay McTighe and Steven Ferrara (https://secureservercdn.net/198.71.233.9/4ba.49d.myftpupload.com/downloads/Assessment-Framework.pdf)
- Resources related to success criteria and rubrics:
    - "Know Your Terms: Analytic, Holistic, and Single-Point Rubrics" by Jennifer Gonzalez (www.cultofpedagogy.com/holistic-analytic-single-point-rubrics/)
    - "What You Need to Know When Establishing Success Criteria in the Classroom" by Kathy Dyer (www.nwea.org/blog/2018/what-you-need-to-know-when-establishing-success-criteria-in-the-classroom/)
    - "Using Success Criteria to Spark Motivation in Your Students" by Marine Freibrun, which includes a post and video (www.teachingchannel.com/blog/success-criteria)

We think it's important to include many learning resources that are easily accessible online, but this also means those resources need to be periodically checked and updated. For our microcredentials, we have a protocol in place to review the resources every six months to make sure the content is still relevant and the sites remain active.

Some microcredential providers have educators work through prescribed online modules with readings and videos that teachers must process as they work to complete a job-embedded task. Although this removes some choice and ownership on the part of those completing a microcredential, it does provide greater structure over the process.

Task

A microcredential's task should encourage educators to apply skills within the context of their classrooms. To that end, a task should include multiple activities that, in combination, demonstrate competence in the skills described by the learning targets. The task should be designed to apply in a variety of contexts, such as grade levels and content areas. This would preclude any task that requires students to submit sample essays, for example, as they wouldn't work well with some grade levels and content areas. This flexibility not only assures that the microcredential will be widely applicable, but also requires users to determine (rather than to be told) how the skill can best be manifested in their specific context, thus supporting the self-directed nature of the microcredential.

Here are some examples of tasks that could be used across a variety of microcredentials and are appropriate for all grade levels and content areas:

- Create instructional plans incorporating a targeted strategy or pedagogy. (We often ask teachers to annotate these plans with observations and reflections related to the skill.)
- Transcribe or record excerpts from classroom learning activities or other interactions where the skill is evident.
- Ask a colleague to observe as you demonstrate the skill, recording data that describes student responses or behaviors.
- Collect data from students (e.g., interviews, exit slips, or surveys) that provide insight about how your use of the skill affected learning.
- Collect and analyze student work samples that show evidence of students' responses to your use of the skill.

Designers sometimes build flexibility into tasks by providing multiple options from which users can choose. In some microcredentials, users design their own tasks, aligning them with the skill and success criteria. Figure 4.4 shows an excerpt from a microcredential that allows participants some choice over the evidence they collect. (See Appendix B for an example from Virginia Beach's social-emotional learning specialization that allows educators to choose their own artifacts showing evidence of the identified learning target.)

FIGURE 4.4

Microcredential with Choice Example

Skill: Integrate scaffolding into project-based learning to strengthen students' work.

Learning Targets

- Choose multiple scaffolding strategies that support a planned project.
- Embed the strategies at appropriate times during instruction and project work.
- Determine and reflect on the connection between planned scaffolds and quality of student work.

Evidence

Option 1:

- Submit a list of three to five scaffolding strategies you will use, the points in the project where you will use each strategy, and your rationale for your choices.
- Submit student artifacts from three individuals or three groups that demonstrate the way that scaffolding supported revision and improvement of the work. Annotate the artifacts *or* provide a written description *or* submit an audio narrative to describe the scaffolding you used in each of the three cases and clarify how the students responded by revising their work. Be sure your selections illustrate more than one type of scaffolding.
- Submit a short narrative in which you reflect on (1) your choices of scaffolding strategies, (2) what you might do differently when using these strategies again, and (3) how you plan to apply any of these strategies in an upcoming lesson or unit.

Option 2:

- Submit a series of lesson plans or an excerpt from a unit plan in which students are working to complete a project over a period of at least five class periods. Highlight examples of scaffolds that will be incorporated.
- Submit three video clips: one from early in the instructional sequence, one near the middle, and one near the end. Each clip should show your use of a scaffolding strategy and include students' responses. Plan so that more than one strategy is shown.
- Submit a short narrative in which you reflect on (1) your choices of scaffolding strategies, (2) what you might do differently when using these strategies again, and (3) how you plan to apply any of these strategies in an upcoming lesson or unit.

Source: VASCD. Used with permission.

> **From the Field: Self-Directed Microcredentials**
>
> For social-emotional learning (SEL) specialization, Virginia Beach City Public Schools allows teachers to select artifacts that demonstrate their understanding of the critical components of SEL, including a supportive classroom environment, explicit instruction, and practice of the skill during academic learning. Each credential in the specialization is based on a specific competency with developmentally aligned skills students demonstrate as they develop socially and emotionally. Teachers choose from a variety of resources, both district-made and external, to learn about and select the skills they would like to emphasize in their practice. As teachers integrate SEL into their classroom, they create their own tasks that demonstrate their understanding and use of the critical components of SEL in the classroom (Angelyn Nichols, personal communication, August 16, 2021).

Reflection

We encourage designers to include opportunities for reflection as part of the task. Our process includes a pre-reflection prior to beginning the new learning to connect to or scaffold prior experiences and also to provide context for the work being completed. The thinking revealed in these short narratives also provides a frame of reference that will be helpful to the person who is assessing or providing feedback on the work.

Here are some examples of pre-reflection questions from a "Building and Using Rubrics" microcredential:

- How do you currently determine whether your students have met their learning goals?
- What kinds of learning targets are best suited to assessment using a rubric?
- In what ways might the use of a rubric benefit student learning?

We also encourage a post-reflection that is designed for practitioners to consider the impact of their new learning on their practice and, ultimately, on student outcomes. Here, for example, are post-reflection questions for the "Building and Using Rubrics" microcredential:

- What was most challenging for you in completing the task?
- Did you learn anything once you began using the rubric that caused you to rethink its design? If so, what do you plan to change and why?
- Did the rubric help you discriminate between degrees of quality of student work? If so, describe what aspect of its design helped you to do so. If not, what might you change to better help you with this?
- Describe one way or one situation in which using the rubric clearly benefited student learning. How will you carry this insight forward in your practice?

To ensure that the task and reflections associated with a microcredential are valid representations of a particular skill or set of skills, we encourage microcredential designers to conduct an alignment check (McTighe et al., 2020). For this activity, designers should share the task and reflections with a colleague who understands the microcredential's topic but who was not directly involved in the design process. Without looking at the learning targets, the colleague should try to infer the skill to which the task and reflections are aligned. If an intended learning target deviates significantly from that identified by the colleague, then revisions to the skill, task, or reflection might be needed.

When developing tasks, consider the key traits *contextual, self-directed, personalized,* and *accessible* and the variables *support/guidance* and *learning resources.* Ensure that it is aligned with the other three components.

Evidence

As with all types of performance assessment, successful completion of a microcredential depends on an examination of evidence provided by the participant showing that the success criteria have been met. This evidence can be examined in any number of ways—by a trained external assessor, by experts within the teacher's school or district, or by colleagues providing feedback to one another within a study group or PLC-type collaborative group.

Regardless of who conducts the examination or how, clear and specific information about what evidence will be accepted should be part of the design process rather than determined on the fly by the teacher or assessor. All learners, including professionals pursuing microcredentials, are more successful when clear expectations are in place. These expectations are communicated primarily through success criteria, but a description or perhaps some examples of the type of evidence to be submitted can also be very helpful as a frame of reference for the learner.

As we've previously noted, some microcredential designs leave the choice of evidence up to the learner, which supports a more self-directed learning experience and provides an opportunity for learner choice. In our work, we have chosen to specify the evidence that is required, in some cases offering a set of predetermined choices. We have found that this helps teachers to feel confident that their evidence has the depth and scope that will be expected. It also allows designers to exert some control over the amount of evidence that will be submitted—enough to sufficiently reflect the success criteria and allow assessors to provide feedback, but also not so much that it overburdens the assessor.

With the exception of written responses to the pre- and post-reflection components of the microcredential, the evidence to be submitted should consist of artifacts that are collected during the course of completing the task. We encourage designers to continually remind themselves that the microcredential is intended to be job-embedded, so anything that is to be submitted for assessment should, to the greatest extent possible, be produced in the course of the practitioner's daily work.

Typical examples of evidence for pedagogical skills include lesson or unit plans (or excerpts from them that demonstrate specific success criteria), transcripts or recordings from a learning activity, and examples of student work. In selecting artifacts that will be used as evidence, designers should keep in mind that the ultimate purpose of completing a microcredential is to benefit student learning.

From the Field: Focusing on Student Impact

Los Angeles Unified's microcredentials include evidence of both designing and implementing project-based learning (PBL). Practitioners

> submit artifacts such as a back-to-school night presentation explaining what PBL is and how it can be used, lesson plans or designed tasks, samples of student work, rubrics containing feedback, or recorded class discussions with reflection questions to help the practitioner understand how the design led to student outcomes (Simone Charles, personal communication, August 23, 2021).

When selecting evidence, consider the key traits *standardized, personalized,* and *valid* and the variables *assessment* and *feedback*. Ensure that it is aligned with the other three components.

The checklist in Appendix C can be used to guide the design of microcredentials as well as to engage in self- and peer review throughout the design process. This way, designers can be sure that their work aligns with the key traits outlined throughout this book while also being a good "fit" for the school, district, or organization based on their needs, resources, and goals. (See Appendix D for an annotated example of a microcredential that addresses the four essential components and highlights the key traits.)

Designing Microcredentials: The Process

As with other types of performance assessment, microcredential designs are not linear. Learning targets will be adjusted as designers wrestle with grain size. Success criteria will be revised as the task comes into focus. Evidence may be modified to better support teacher reflection. Internal and external reviewers may notice inconsistencies or potential points of confusion. These "mid-design" decisions are to be expected and will help to strengthen the microcredential and the impact it will have on educators and students.

The following decisions should be made prior to launching the design process.

Who Will Lead the Process?

Designing viable microcredentials that achieve the goals you have selected is a complex process. Even before the process begins, it is important to decide who will facilitate and direct the many aspects involved in creating the microcredentials. At a minimum, the individual tasked with leading the process should have a strong understanding of the content of the microcredentials to be designed, as well as an understanding of how any proposed microcredentials align with the mission or goals of the district or school.

Because the design will likely involve several people and multiple drafts, the leader must be prepared to provide the coordination the process requires. It is also important that this facilitator have the respect and trust of those involved. If human capital is spread thin within a district, then adopting existing microcredentials might be a more viable option.

> **From the Field: Leading the Process**
>
> In Albemarle, an equity specialist gathered research on and successful examples of culturally responsive teaching from the teaching community, then partnered with other educator leaders to launch their own culturally responsive teaching microcredential that aligned with their equity-based policies, mission, and goals (Lars Holmstrom, personal communication, June 25, 2021).
>
>
>
> Virginia Beach uses existing teacher leadership teams of "design fellows" who commit to specializing in a particular topic for a year or more. These design fellows may develop a microcredential then implement it in their own classrooms. They can also potentially serve as evaluators of microcredential tasks going forward (Janene Gorham, personal communication, May 14, 2021).

Who Will Design the Microcredential?

Some school districts may rely on curriculum specialists or supervisors to design their microcredentials. Alternatively, teams of teachers with particular areas of expertise may be selected. In the case of VASCD, which is a statewide professional association rather than a school district, we identified interested members from across Virginia who had both the expertise and willingness to engage in an authoring process that included drafts, feedback, and revisions. In other instances, outside consultants might be engaged as designers.

Who Will Be in Charge of Training?

Designers must be trained in how to properly design microcredentials. This training can come from outside experts (as in our case) or from in-house experts who have researched a variety of microcredentials. At a minimum, an effective training session should include the following components:

- Reviewing what a microcredential is and is not
- Explaining key components of a microcredential and how to design them
- Time for reflection and practice
- Sharing drafts for feedback

> ### From the Field: Training
>
> In our case, Sue Z. Beers, executive director of Members Impacting Students; Improving Curriculum (MISIC), provided training for us. Sue shared the template that MISIC was using at that time, explained the rationale behind each section of the template, and then led us through the writing of a microcredential. In our training, we produced our first drafts of microcredentials, and Sue provided us with expert feedback. While not everyone who participated in our training sessions became a microcredential designer, the training provided us with common understandings and language for use by designers, reviewers, and practitioners.

How and by Whom Will the Microcredential Be Reviewed?

Our review process includes both internal and external reviews. When a draft of a microcredential is complete, it is first reviewed by two or more members of our team who were not involved in the drafting process. They look for evidence of the quality criteria, check the alignment to key components, and provide proofreading and editing help. They also assess the appropriateness and reasonableness of the activities. When they are done, they return the microcredential to the authors with specific suggestions, comments, and questions that often result in revisions. Following revision, the microcredential is sent to at least two external reviewers who have agreed to evaluate it using a checklist like the one in Appendix E and to provide any additional comments. These external reviews are done by practitioners who can predict potential concerns, challenges, or confusion on the part of microcredential users.

After a final review by the permanent writing group, our completed microcredentials are field-tested by volunteer educators who receive credit for them and agree to provide feedback both on the design process and on the microcredentials themselves. This gives us valuable information and allows us to address any concerns related to both design and implementation before other educators participate.

If your school or district is interested in microcredentials for educators, you may decide to search for them from outside providers or engage internal staff in a design process. Either way, we recommend that you review each of the essential components (learning targets, success criteria, learning resources, task, and evidence) to ensure that they are aligned, use success criteria as indicators of quality, and consider the variables and design process decisions outlined above. As the adoption or design process begins to take shape, the implementation process then should kick into gear. The next chapter examines some considerations for schools, districts, or organizations as they roll out microcredentials.

5

Implementing a Microcredentialing Process

Like many districts, Virginia Beach had a largely prescriptive and compliance-oriented professional development program. As classroom instruction and student learning increasingly focused on agency, personalized learning, and choice, it became clear to the Office of Professional Growth and Innovation that the district was not emphasizing the same kinds of learning goals for teachers, such as a more personalized approach to professional learning. What started as an interest in changing the professional development conversation from a fixation on license renewal points to a focus on the actual impact of PD on learning became a multiyear journey toward a robust microcredentialing program.

Teachers in Virginia Beach have numerous professional learning resources and opportunities, but the district wanted to find a way to formalize a personalized learning process for educators that included some kind of recognition with an emphasis on the demonstration of learning and transfer to the classroom. They recognized that teachers could take whatever they learned, however they learned it, and apply it to classroom practice. However, teachers were asking to receive points for all kinds of learning experiences, from Twitter chats to independent research projects. Through those requests, questions began to surface: What does it mean to be a professional teacher? What really matters in terms of professional learning? How do professional development experiences help teachers learn in ways that change their practice? How can they demonstrate this change? The district wanted to trust teachers to guide decisions about their learning without being told what to take.

At the same time, the district was working to develop a career lattice for teachers. The lattice, as opposed to a more traditional ladder, allows educators to demonstrate nonlinear growth in areas of interest. The district wondered: How do we help teachers who have been in the career for a while feel that they are being recognized for their expertise and remain motivated to grow and learn? Simply acquiring continuing education units was not doing that. The answer for Virginia Beach was specializations, which represent a deep dive into a topic that focuses on some aspect of professional practice. And the mechanism for formally assessing the specialization was a microcredential (Janene Gorham, personal communication, May 14, 2021).

Implementing Microcredentials

As we showed in Chapters 3 and 4, selecting and designing microcredentials requires care, attention, and strategic decision making. However, as the example above reminds us, no matter how high the quality, microcredentials will not have a positive effect on teaching and learning without an effective implementation strategy. Effective implementation requires careful consideration of a variety of factors, including who should participate in the microcredentials, how and when microcredentials should be implemented, and how microcredentials will be assessed. In this chapter, we share a variety of tips and questions to consider while making these considerations. The answers to many of the questions will be determined by the unique resources, needs, and goals of those planning and engaging in these learning experiences.

Determining Participants

When you know *who* will be completing the microcredentials, it is easier to determine *how* to effectively implement a microcredentialing program. The intended audience will help guide the level of support provided, inform whether educators will complete the credentials independently in a self-directed way, and determine how long it should take to complete each microcredential.

Novice teachers can complete microcredentials as part of an induction program, choosing specific skills in collaboration with a mentor or coach. Microcredentials can validate what they have learned during their induction period, offering novice teachers an opportunity to apply and demonstrate their skills in meaningful ways. Proficient teachers can select specific skills they would like to develop further, seeking feedback from evaluators who can support their deepening understanding of advanced pedagogical concepts and skills. Teachers on improvement plans can find targeted support by selecting a microcredential that addresses an area for improvement, seeking coaching and feedback related to a specific student learning outcome.

In cases where the approach is centralized (see Chapter 2), a target audience for microcredentials may already be evident. If not, then it's important to determine who specifically will complete the microcredential. Will it be individual teachers self-selecting to participate? Will it be grade- or subject-level teams? Will a whole faculty or district work together to complete microcredentials to meet a specific goal? What will motivate participants to value the work required of the microcredential? Establishing a purpose for completing the credential is essential when selecting a target audience and strategy.

When selecting who will complete the microcredential, it is important to consider why teachers might be motivated to accept the challenge: "To build educators' ability to develop students' literacy skills, language arts specialists or coaches may be the first to complete the microcredentials, anticipating that they will then help to support others in the process," for example, or "To qualify for a continuing contract during their probation period."

A centralized approach does not necessarily preclude providing educators with the choice to opt into the process. When asked why he decided to complete a specialization, Virginia Beach teacher Anthony Nobles said, "For me, it was about personal goal setting and working toward something, plus the opportunity to collaborate with other educators" (personal communication, May 25, 2021). At the same time, building capacity to meet organizational goals often suggests a more strategic approach that considers needed supports, timing, and microcredential assessment.

Piloting Microcredentials

Even if districts or schools elect to adopt existing microcredentials, they may consider piloting these with a group of educators prior to implementation. In our experience, this provides useful information to help guide the full-scale implementation decisions discussed in this chapter. In the case of VASCD, our piloting process involved recruiting volunteers from our membership who had expressed interest in learning more about microcredentialing by signing on as participants. These volunteers chose among a group of about a dozen microcredentials, selecting skills that would legitimately align with and strengthen their practice. During the microcredentialing process, and then again when teachers had completed it, we solicited feedback through both surveys and phone interviews. The comments provided by these volunteers gave us valuable insight on areas where, for example, directions needed to be clearer and success criteria more explicit.

> **From the Field: Piloting Microcredentials**
>
> At Norwalk, administrators picked a specific school to implement the microcredentials first so that examples generated from these initial participants could be used when the credentials become available to a wider audience. The school was chosen because of its prior experience and training in project-based learning (PBL), which was the subject of the microcredentials (Tina Henckel, personal communication, June 17, 2021).
>
>
>
> Los Angeles Unified is starting its own PBL microcredentialing efforts with alternative high schools because the teachers and administrators have a specific problem to solve: engaging students who are not succeeding in a traditional school environment. The pilot schools plan to share their successes and challenges with other high schools and career and technical education programs, adding future PBL cohorts (Simone Charles, personal communication, August 23, 2021).
>
>
>
> Richardson ISD started with four campuses to test out each credential. District leaders believed it was very important to get the launch of their microcredentials right, recognizing how difficult it can be to reframe the way teachers view professional learning (Tabitha Branum, personal communication, May 21, 2021).

Implementation Support

Different levels of support will be needed based on the expertise of each microcredential participant. Some teachers may be able to complete a microcredential without any further support because they have extensive knowledge and application experience. At the same time, it is important to avoid what is known as "unconscious competence" (Aguilar, 2018), which is when a teacher is able to use a skill without effort. Over time, teachers may lose their ability to transfer the skill to new contexts if they do not have explicit practice and opportunity to talk about the skill with others. On the other hand, when teachers are "consciously competent" (Aguilar, 2018), they know the skills they have acquired, they can reflect on their growth, and they can describe their skills to others in meaningful ways.

Other teachers may be actively acquiring and transferring skills while they are completing a microcredential, working to develop conscious competence. They are likely to take advantage of resources provided and may also seek additional learning opportunities, such as through traditional courses or from a coach, to demonstrate their new understanding. Teachers at this level may be skilled at finding resources and making connections for themselves as they move toward conscious competence, but others may need support acquiring the knowledge and skills necessary to successfully complete the credential.

> ### From the Field: Implementation Support
>
> One Virginia Beach teacher, Jenn Vedder, chose to complete a microcredential on building a classroom community.
>
> "I selected the credential because this is something I have been working on for a couple of years now," she said. "Because of the hybrid environment I was teaching in, I was 100 percent committed to really focusing on this. I was wondering what classroom community looks like, sounds like, and feels like in a virtual setting. I wanted to know, 'Am I doing this right?'"
>
> Vedder enlisted the support of one of the literacy coaches at her school because "I needed someone to flesh out ideas with, and she

helped me choose the one that really showed how I was building classroom community and how I was really attempting to engage learners. I found her input vital to the process because she knows how important it is to have a sense of community before students can even begin to process what you are teaching them" (personal communication, May 27, 2021).

According to Virginia Beach Director of Professional Growth and Innovation Janene Gorham, the microcredential process is "a way for educators to get validated for something they do regularly that may never be measured in any way—something that is a best practice. Microcredentials are a good way for teachers to take a look at what they're doing to refine it to make it even better for students because somebody is looking at their work" (personal communication, May 14, 2021).

For its project-based learning (PBL) microcredentials, Los Angeles Unified began the process by providing training on what PBL looks like and how teachers can design high-quality PBL experiences. After teachers designed their tasks, the microcredential required them to articulate their design decisions and how they aligned to the characteristics of high-quality PBL, increasing participants' depth of understanding and likelihood of transfer as they moved toward conscious competence throughout the process (Simone Charles, personal communication, August 23, 2021).

The option to complete a microcredential independently appeals to many educators, but these same educators also appreciate knowing that they have available support when they need it. In our first year of microcredential implementation, practitioners from 13 school districts participated. Two of these districts had a central office member who monitored teachers' progress, periodically touching base with them via email about their completion schedule and offering encouragement. These districts were the only two in which every teacher who enrolled also completed the microcredential successfully.

Working toward a microcredential as a member of a professional learning community or cohort can deepen teachers' professional learning and maximize the chances that the learning will last. For example, in both Albemarle and Norwalk, teachers complete their microcredentials in cohorts. They are encouraged to meet regularly with others from their cohort to share experiences, ideas, and questions. In a project involving teachers from across five districts, a cohort model was shown to contribute to teacher satisfaction with the learning experience: "Teachers who pursued their computational thinking microcredentials in peer cohorts pointed to this collaboration as integral to their learning. Among participating teachers surveyed, collaborative planning time with colleagues was the top support, cited by roughly three-quarters (74 percent) of the respondents" (Luke & Young, n.d., p. 7).

It is important to consider how much support to provide for completing the microcredentials. Will teachers be given a timeline with deadlines for various checkpoints? For example, teachers may be required to check in with an evaluator or coach after answering focus questions at the beginning of a credential to make sure they have a clear understanding of a skill before moving on to more explicit activities. Consideration should also be given to whether teachers will be allowed to complete the credential at any time or if there will be set starting and stopping times (for the sake of evaluation or awarding of points), as well as to whether any parts of the microcredential will be required for completion, such as a specific reading activity or type of submission.

From the Field: Determining Appropriate Levels of Support

Virginia Beach continues to wrestle with how much support to give teachers. The district does not want teachers to feel alone or to struggle. At the same time, administrators hope to meet teachers' needs without giving unequal assistance that could create variable levels of competence once a badge is awarded. The district ensures consistency in each microcredential through clear articulation of the competency and a well-defined rubric with clear criteria. Teachers and anyone

> supporting them can thus measure themselves against the rubric to guide their learning. Sometimes traditional classes related to the microcredential topics are offered to support teachers if they want a more guided experience, but course completion does not automatically lead to a badge. Instead, the course gives teachers knowledge they must apply, and the artifact they submit demonstrates that application (see Appendix B) (Janene Gorham, personal communication, May 14, 2021).

Assessing Microcredentials and Providing Feedback

One of the most challenging and rewarding parts of microcredential implementation is assessing the credential and providing feedback to the teacher. In Chapter 2, we discussed the importance of feedback in helping educators complete microcredentials. Here, we share some specific tips for assessors. It is rare for educators to get feedback on their work outside scheduled performance evaluations, and many are eager to hear what others think about the work that means the most to them. To make the microcredentialing experience meaningful for teachers, leaders will need to consider how to make sure teachers completely understand what the credential is asking them to learn and be able to do. One way is to include checkpoints through the microcredentialing process in the form of formative assessments.

Another consideration is how to structure the assessment process. How will reliability be ensured? Will there be multiple reviewers? Do assessors need to calibrate their scores with a sample credential? And how will assessors be trained?

There are many things that should be included in assessor training. It can be tempting to get lost in the logistical details of timelines and how to use scoring tools when the quality of feedback is just as important. Whether intended for students or adult learners, effective feedback should be

1. Goal-referenced,
2. Tangible and transparent,
3. Actionable,

4. User-friendly,
5. Timely,
6. Ongoing, and
7. Consistent. (Wiggins, 2012)

To support teachers as they work through their microcredentials, instructional coaches, teacher leaders, and other colleagues can be deployed to provide feedback along the way. They may check in with participants at structured intervals, record and debrief lessons, or critique an artifact before it is submitted. Coaches may also use microcredentials as a common assessment for the teachers they are coaching, asking teachers to complete them as tangible evidence of understanding of the skill or skills for which they are receiving coaching. Instructional coaches can also assess the final work, though it may be advantageous for districts to use external assessors in order to save time, provide validation, or ensure that coaching and evaluation are conducted by different parties.

Figure 5.1 shows a few examples of high-quality feedback that was provided to some of the practitioners completing VASCD microcredentials. Each example includes the microcredential topic, example feedback, and a brief explanation of why that feedback is effective.

Accessibility

To ensure that microcredentials can be self-directed and completed at the educator's own pace, they should be accessible at any time from any location. Learning management systems, which are already used by almost all schools and districts, can be effective not only for housing microcredentials but also as conduits through which teachers can submit their work and receive feedback from assessors. When identifying and selecting a platform to house a microcredential, schools or districts should consider its cost, how easy it is for educators to use, and (where applicable) whether it allows for direct access on the part of an external assessor.

Schools or districts may also want to explore the possibility of using sites that allow for the design and awarding of digital badges. Such badges should align with the skill or skills being mastered and provide both a written summary of the completed work as well as a visual representation of completion. Educators often display these badges around their classrooms or on their social media platforms to signal to parents, colleagues, and administrators that they are a go-to source for a given topic or skill. In addition, Gamrat and Zimmerman (2021) note that digital badges can be used to support future decisions about professional learning. For example, earning a microcredential and digital badge related to performance task design might signal the need for additional learning around this larger topic. It makes intuitive sense that once an educator learns more about the design of actual performance tasks, they may recognize a need for additional professional learning around rubrics, for example, to evaluate student work from these performance tasks.

FIGURE 5.1

Effective Feedback Examples

Microcredential Topic	Feedback	Why the Feedback Is Effective
Building classroom community	*Success Criterion* The strategy being used by students in the video aligns with one of the lesson plans submitted and demonstrates students applying the strategy after practice and feedback. *Assessor's Feedback* Meets criteria: You were able to show through your video the use of the "teammates consult" strategy. I appreciated how you left one group of students in the "main room" in order to show how quick the discussions went. I would be excited to see how this strategy would transfer to in-person teaching and if that would change the level of interaction between the students.	The feedback acknowledges tangible actions from the practitioner's submission that demonstrate students applying the strategy. It also suggests a future application of the strategy that would require the practitioner to transfer understanding to an in-person session in an actionable way.

Microcredential Topic	Feedback	Why the Feedback Is Effective
Creating opportunities for students to cultivate empathy	*Success Criterion* Student work samples or recordings of students demonstrate their understanding of the role of empathy in solving problems. *Assessor's Feedback* Meets criteria: "Students were able to more deeply understand multiple historical perspectives as well as the cause-and-effect relationship between the success of the growing colonies and the demise of indigenous life, land, and culture and to make personal connections to their own lived experiences." The narrative, including this sentence, shows how you clearly incorporated cultivation of empathy to enhance student understanding of the essential knowledge for this lesson/project.	The feedback quotes how and when the students' work samples demonstrated their understanding of the intended goal.
Providing feedback to foster deeper learning	*Success Criterion* Annotations on lessons/activities provide examples of student responses to feedback and link these examples to teacher assessment of effectiveness. *Assessor's Feedback* Meets criteria: I can see evidence of students updating their responses based on your feedback on several of the examples you provided. The summaries were helpful for navigating your artifacts, particularly the ones where you copied and pasted your feedback and the changes the students made. I was not able to see the responses on Flipgrid, but I imagine feedback given there influenced student work in addition to the written feedback you provided. One challenge when giving feedback is knowing when students meet the criteria. I notice your comments generally said "Good" in those instances. Is there some way to give positive feedback that also generates new learning or validates the learning beyond compliance? This may lead to even deeper learning in your classroom.	The submission meets criteria, and the feedback acknowledges how and when the provided examples demonstrated response to feedback. Additionally, the feedback provides a timely, actionable suggestion for a future opportunity to grow further in the skill.

continued

FIGURE 5.1 *continued*
Effective Feedback Examples

Microcredential Topic	Feedback	Why the Feedback Is Effective
Designing a rubric	*Success Criterion* The rubric includes clear evidence of student-friendly language, differences between levels of proficiency, and descriptors that provide opportunities for students to adjust their work to reach higher levels of proficiency. *Assessor's Feedback* Resubmission required: Students are likely able to easily understand the rubric language, but the descriptors need to be more specific and differentiated from each other in order for students to use them for goal setting or revising their work. Consider looking at pieces of student work that you scored at each level and teasing out some of the features that they have in common. Then, ask yourself, would these help you write rubric language that would give students some guidance?	The submission does not meet criteria, and the feedback points out the area in which revision is needed. The assessor also provides a specific suggestion that may be helpful to the educator in revising the work.

Timing

Ideally, teachers will choose and complete a microcredential at a time when it can be naturally embedded in their practice. Schools or districts may also consider how a microcredential fits into a larger strategy, goal, or initiative when choosing when teachers should complete the microcredential. For example, teachers may need to have a basic understanding of rubric design before participating in a curriculum writing project hosted by the district.

The timing of microcredentials may also be linked to the plan for assessing them and to the number of assessors available. And if the credential is linked to continuing education units, it may need to be completed before points are submitted for the school year.

> ### From the Field: Timing
>
> In Virginia Beach, teacher Anthony Nobles selected a microcredential about the classroom environment to be completed at the beginning of a semester when building community is especially important. "I don't think secondary teachers prioritize the learning environment like they should," he said, "so I thought my efforts could move secondary teachers in that direction" (personal communication, May 25, 2021). In this way, Nobles saw completing the microcredential as an opportunity for leadership in addition to personal growth.
>
>
>
> At Albemarle, where a focus on equity is ingrained in the district's mission, a monthly cohort meeting is held for educators interested in completing their culturally responsive teaching microcredential. Educators are encouraged to begin the microcredential process early in the year and to participate regularly in these monthly meetings. The district essentially gives educators a year to complete the microcredential so they can have ample time to implement and reflect on new practices (Lars Holmstrom, personal communication, June 25, 2021).

Planning for microcredential implementation can help districts and schools avoid pitfalls that have the potential to derail the process. We recommend at least a small pilot project prior to full implementation, as we have found that this is helpful for revealing and ironing out problems prior to full-scale use. In the next chapter, we will discuss the role of leadership in supporting implementation of microcredentials.

6

Leading for Success

So far in this book, we have focused largely on the ways that educators access and engage with high-quality microcredentials. We've provided examples illustrating a variety of current approaches and noted the importance of aligning decisions about microcredentialing to goals through a theory of action. We've discussed what to look for in microcredentials, how school districts might design their own, and issues related to implementation. In this chapter, we zoom out from the more technical aspects of microcredential design and implementation to examine some of the ways that education leaders and policymakers can successfully support microcredentialing programs.

We believe that microcredentials can help elevate and revitalize professional learning in education, creating more meaningful, relevant, and student-centered learning experiences for educators—but only if we decide that the highest-quality professional learning will also be our highest priority. We envision an education landscape in which microcredentials are not "extras" to be used after compliance-based professional learning requirements have been met through hours counted and points accrued. Rather, we see microcredentialing as a part of every educator's professional growth over the course of a career—a tool that can be used whenever it aligns with individual, school, or district goals. This approach must be embraced by school, district, and state educational leaders if microcredentialing is to fulfill its promise. Leaders who advocate for microcredentialing, even those who acknowledge they have yet to perfect the process, should be willing to commit to building a stronger bridge from professional learning to teacher proficiency and student success.

A Shared Definition of Microcredentials

In order for microcredentials to become a widely accepted model for professional learning, a common definition is needed. We have suggested that a microcredential must contain certain key components and qualities (see Chapter 1). Our definition of a microcredential—*a performance-based assessment intended to allow the educator to demonstrate competency in a skill*—is informed by what we know about professional learning that impacts practice. It takes advantage of the way in which microcredentials can guide educators not only in gaining new knowledge, but also in applying that knowledge to their practice and understanding how changes to their practice influence student learning.

We believe that the key components and quality criteria we describe in this book are important to realizing the potential of microcredentialing, but ours is not the only approach, nor are we suggesting it is the only "correct" one. That said, it is imperative that the profession agree on what is (and is not) a microcredential; *in our view, all microcredentials must, at the very minimum, be clearly competency-based, requiring demonstration of proficiency and benefit to student learning in an authentic context*. Without a common understanding of what a microcredential is, the effectiveness of this powerful professional learning model will be diluted and eventually lost.

In 2020, the Council of Chief State School Officers issued a report from a task force convened in cooperation with Digital Promise to address the need for "greater consistency, relevance, and rigor among micro-credential offerings" (p. 5). The report includes design, assessment, and implementation principles that largely reflect the considerations described throughout this book. Further, the review cites the need for "micro-credentials to be reviewed by a qualified, objective third party" (p. 5). We agree that a quality-control process guided by agreed-upon principles is essential to realizing the potential benefits of microcredentials.

School Leadership

Clear communication and appropriate incentives (often from the district) are necessary to inform educators and motivate them to participate in microcredentialing. Leaders at the school level must then plan the ways in which microcredentials can be leveraged to reap the greatest advantages in the contexts of their individual schools. One of these advantages is the opportunity for focused, productive collaboration around shared professional learning goals. Unlike a certification exam or a paper written for a graduate course, the microcredentialing process allows for colleagues to work together. Just as a team of students may brainstorm or practice together prior to completing a performance assessment, educators may find it helpful to consult with coaches or other colleagues as they prepare to tackle microcredential tasks. However, in the final analysis, it is the individual's competency that is assessed, so in order for assessment results to be valid, educators must individually generate and submit evidence to document their skills.

Keeping in mind the necessity for each individual seeking a microcredential to independently demonstrate and document their skills, here are some ways that education leaders might employ microcredentials as focal points for professional learning while integrating various types of collegial supports.

Microcredentialing can be embedded as a strategy within the required process guiding teacher growth. Participation in a microcredential can help to steer professional goal setting away from "what I was going to do anyway" or "what would be easiest" toward more meaningful engagement.

For example, before the beginning of the school year, the principal or assistant principal meets with each teacher to create a professional learning plan that is required as part of the teacher evaluation process. As part of this plan, teachers set professional learning goals that both reflect a need or interest of the individual teacher and align with the school's strategic plan. Some of these professional learning goals are reflected in a collection of microcredentials that are available within the district. Teachers who choose to work toward these microcredentials determine themselves whether to have their work externally evaluated or simply reviewed by the principal. In either case, the microcredential provides an evidence-based way of determining the extent to which the teacher's goal has been met.

Coaches can address the credential directly and provide support to teachers on their own terms. This provides an avenue for increasing trust and a sense of shared responsibility for student learning outcomes.

For example, an instructional coach regularly works with teachers, using the microcredential's success criteria and learning resources to provide starting points and direction for their collaborative work. Though teachers may decide to have their evidence externally assessed, this is not the focus. Rather, the microcredential becomes a tool for the coaches as they work side-by-side with teachers (Sue Z. Beers, personal communication, August 12, 2021).

Teachers can complete microcredentials as a group. Teacher teams or cohorts can implement specific practices from a microcredential in their classrooms and discuss results, reflecting individually while building efficacy collectively. A common concern for teachers completing individual professional development is that the experience can be isolating. Completing the credential with colleagues gives a sense of community. Teams can work together toward a common goal, and evaluated credentials can validate the professional growth that comes from working on a common problem together. Teachers can learn to value the learning process in addition to the outcomes they achieve together.

For example, a professional learning community determines a shared focus for the school year, and members agree to use a microcredential as the basis of their work together. Members of the group individually explore some of the provided learning resources, then share ideas relevant to their context in their regular team meetings. As they prepare for the performance task, they compare notes and plan collaboratively, just as they normally would. As the work progresses, they bring samples of student work to the table for analysis and reflection. Their application of the strategy described in the microcredential is refined and becomes an ongoing aspect of their instruction.

All teachers in a school can work on specific learning goals simultaneously, ensuring that professional development is targeted and meaningful. A microcredential can provide a common language, timeline, and opportunities for strategic support from coaches and administrators. Completed credentials can become tangible evidence of success both for individual teachers and for the faculty as a whole.

For example, student achievement data in a school reveal a pattern that indicates a need for professional learning across the faculty in an area of emphasis. Knowing the importance of growth in this area for all teachers, but also understanding that there are varying levels of expertise among the faculty, the school offers the related microcredential as an alternative to attending "professional learning days" for a semester. Some teachers participate in presentations and workshops on these days, which have been built into the school calendar. Those choosing the microcredential may opt out of the professional learning day activities to work on the credential individually or with a partner as they embed the professional learning in their day-to-day work.

A principal can recommend a microcredential as part of a teacher's performance improvement plan. It can be challenging for principals to provide helpful feedback and support to teachers while serving as their evaluator. In some cases, a microcredential can focus the support a teacher needs while also contributing an external assessment of evidence to the evaluation process.

For example, a principal checks in frequently as the teacher progresses through a microcredential, providing descriptive and corrective feedback and directing the teacher's attention to applicable learning resources. When the teacher's evidence of competency is gathered, it is reviewed by an objective, external assessor to determine the extent to which success criteria have been met. This feedback then becomes part of the data that inform decisions about the teacher's next steps in improvement (Sue Z. Beers, personal communication, August 12, 2021).

School leaders can use microcredentials to anchor book studies. Book studies are a common professional learning tool that can be implemented schoolwide or with teams of educators. To help translate theory or research into practice, school leaders can use microcredentials that ask educators to implement tools or strategies focused on the content that teachers are reading about.

For example, walkthrough data reveal a need for more reading and writing across the curriculum, so a middle school principal decides to have her teachers read a book filled with research-based practices to address this need. To encourage teachers to implement these strategies, she also has them complete a microcredential on the same topic. She and her administrative team review teacher work and hold follow-up meetings to debrief faculty on the impact of the practices.

School leaders have enormous influence over what and how teachers learn. Understanding the variety of ways microcredentials can be used equips leaders to knit microcredentials into their existing practice such that they strengthen teacher effectiveness and make professional learning more meaningful.

District Leadership

Districts must consistently communicate and demonstrate a commitment to teacher quality and to meaningful, productive professional learning. Further, they should consider the costs and benefits of various types of professional learning experiences.

We are occasional attendees and presenters at both state and national conferences. We go to and conduct workshops. We value these experiences, as they expose us to new ideas and expand our networks. However, those of us who have been district administrators know that the return on investment in these activities is typically minimal if measured by transfer of skills into practice (Gulamhussein, 2013). In our interviews for this book, we found examples of school districts that provide incentives and supports so that educators not only reap intrinsic rewards from their microcredential work, but also see concrete benefits to their participation.

In Chapter 2, we discussed the importance of feedback and personalization to help secure buy-in and follow-through on the part of educators completing a microcredential. Here we take this approach one step further, examining specific systems and structures that district leaders can and should leverage to incentivize educators not only to begin the process of microcredentialing, but to complete it as well.

District Incentives and Supports

A common thread among the districts discussed in this book is a need to incentivize educators to complete microcredentials. Even when microcredentials align with district goals or mission statements, it's not enough simply to float the idea of engaging in them to educators without understanding, context, or any incentives. Teachers who have become accustomed to accumulating credits, points, or hours as ways of documenting their professional learning may understandably question a shift to a more competency-based approach.

Without ample and clear information, the ability to exercise choice, and access to support, many teachers will be hesitant to jump into the microcredentialing process. In our own initial conversations with educators, we've heard comments like "I don't need this for my license," "If this is a course, where's my instructor?" and "What do I get if I pass?"

There are many outcomes an individual practitioner may be seeking when deciding to complete a microcredential, including personal or professional growth, personalized feedback, and improved student outcomes. Although we would like to believe that intrinsic motivation and the joy of learning would be enough to compel teachers to participate in microcredentials, we are also realistic. Over the years, teachers have become accustomed to compliance-based professional learning. The connection between professional learning experiences and daily practice is often tenuous, so it's understandable that educators would be skeptical about taking on a project that adds to their demanding workload. In addition, many educators can readily give examples of trends that have come and gone from their school districts without leaving a lasting impact. They have learned the hard way that investing in a new initiative isn't always rewarded.

Participation in microcredentials requires more self-motivation than, say, attending a workshop, so districts should consider what tools they have at their disposal for motivating their educators to complete them. Here are some possible examples.

Career ladders and lattices. Microcredentials can be a part of district support for career advancement and enhancement. Whether the focus is on educators' opportunities to move into leadership roles (career ladder) or broaden the scope of their expertise (career lattices), documentation of their proficiency is a helpful component:

- In Virginia Beach, teachers can include microcredential artifacts and badges when applying for positions in central office to demonstrate that they understand district-level goals like technology integration, social-emotional learning, equity, and performance-based learning (Janene Gorham, personal communication, May 14, 2021).
- In Los Angeles Unified, teachers can earn professional learning points that reflect the growth and learning they have demonstrated through microcredentials. These professional learning points then factor into promotions when teachers apply for advancement into roles such as curriculum and instructional coaches, specialists, or administrators (Simone Charles, personal communication, August 23, 2021).

Stipends and raises. Financial incentives are one way to motivate educators to complete microcredentials. These can take the form of one-time stipends or raises in exchange for completing one or more microcredentials:

- In Albemarle, teachers are given a one-time stipend to complete their culturally responsive teaching microcredential (Lars Holmstrom, personal communication, June 25, 2021).
- Richardson ISD determines levels of effectiveness using evidence from classroom instruction in the form of badges that equate to hours. Teachers determine how many badges they would like to earn based on the number of hours they are aiming for. The more hours they complete, the higher the level of effectiveness they demonstrate, which leads to a salary increase (Tabitha Branum, personal communication, May 21, 2021).
- Los Angeles Unified offers teachers the option to earn salary credits or professional development pay for each credential earned (Simone Charles, personal communication, August 23, 2021).

Time. Districts can work with teachers to free up time so that they can fully invest in the application and reflection necessary for success:

- Los Angeles Unified provides time for teachers to complete their credentials both during and outside contracted hours. The school site administrator makes time in the schedule and compensates teachers for any time they spend outside their normal teaching responsibilities completing microcredentials (Simone Charles, personal communication, August 23, 2021).
- In lieu of attending otherwise required activities and meetings on professional development days, two Iowa districts offered every teacher in the district the opportunity to choose three microcredentials to complete from a stack of seven related to an area of general district professional development need. The districts covered the cost of external evaluations. Teachers who successfully completed the customized stacks of microcredentials received one licensure renewal credit from the state's Board of Education Examiners. Staff from the building and district offices checked in with teachers along the way and provided support for their work. Professional learning communities also worked together to share

their learning and to provide input on one another's work (Sue Z. Beers, personal communication, August 12, 2021).

Coaching and collegial support. Districts can deploy support professionals to schools and track implementation progress based on intended outcomes, creating tangible evidence of progress toward a specific goal. This helps educators understand their individual roles in the larger plan and allows them to chart their own pathway toward meeting that plan:

- Richardson ISD assigns leaders to support practitioners working on microcredentials. The leaders check in periodically with participants and make it clear they are available if anyone needs help. They also periodically create synchronous and asynchronous content and post resources participants may find useful. These actions show participants that the leaders are responsive to their needs and reading their submissions in progress along the way (Tabitha Branum, personal communication, May 21, 2021).
- Norwalk provides professional development time for practitioners to work together on microcredentials throughout the school year. With support from district and building leaders, participants can ask questions and gather evidence during work hours. Providing time during the workday demonstrates that leaders are committed to microcredential completion and gives participants time to reflect on their practice and meet microcredential requirements (Tina Henckel, personal communication, June 17, 2021).
- Winchester asks its computer science integration coaches to support elementary teachers as they work on computer science microcredentials. The coaches first orient the teachers to the site that is providing the microcredential and make sure they are clear about what is required for completion. Then they may talk the teachers through their ideas about how to meet those requirements, brainstorming lessons that might demonstrate their competency. Depending on the teacher's knowledge and comfort, a coach may come in and model the use of a coding device or build the teacher's and students' understanding of computational thinking through a variety of activities. Finally, the coach may read over a lesson the teacher is preparing or assist with filming on the day the

teacher wants to video their teaching. Additionally, coaches may spend time reflecting with the teacher on their evidence before they submit (Amy Thomas, personal communication, May 25, 2021).

State Leadership

State-level leadership and policies can also encourage teachers, schools, or districts to pursue microcredentials as professional learning models or even as pathways to endorsement or relicensure.

For example, in 2019, the Virginia General Assembly enacted legislation that allows microcredentialing for endorsement in STEM areas, where teacher shortages are a concern. As policymakers work to update teacher licensure regulations, Virginia Department of Education staff are investigating the potential for microcredentialing in additional content areas. Similar efforts are underway in several other states as well, such as Kentucky, North Carolina, Tennessee, Wisconsin, and Utah, to name a few, where the competency-based nature of microcredentials is seen as a way to make professional learning more meaningful, accessible, and relevant to practice (ExcelinEd, 2019). As DeMonte (2017) notes,

> For states, micro-credentials have noteworthy benefits. For one, states can more easily offer micro-credentials that are aligned with teaching standards and other state initiatives (for example, to support efforts to help all teachers develop the skills needed to teach English language learners). For another, micro-credential training is often delivered online, meaning it can be more accessible to rural educators and those who need to engage in professional learning in the evening, on weekends, or during school breaks. Lastly, states using micro-credentials demonstrate their support for educators' abilities to understand their own professional learning needs. (p. 2)

From the Field: State Policy

Davis School District in Utah launched its own competency-based professional learning initiative in 2017 and quickly began collaborating with the Utah State Board of Education (USBE) to develop a working prototype using a platform that was already providing state transcription services for teachers. By 2019, educators around the state were earning

> microcredentials. The Davis School District's initiative supported the USBE's focus on competency-based professional learning and provided an additional pathway to endorsement. Staff at the state level created microcredentials that could replace courses provided by higher education institutions, and eventually integrated microcredentials into both relicensure and endorsement. Although microcredentials are not mandated by the state, many school districts provide a salary increase when a stack or certain number of microcredentials has been completed.
>
> Microcredentials in the USBE's web-based catalog are developed in partnership with Utah districts, charters, regional service centers, higher education institutions, the Utah Education Network, and other stakeholders in Utah's public education system. A state microcredential advisory committee provides final approval of all microcredentials and awards USBE credits. The successful use of microcredentials in Utah has led to discussions about a possible collaboration with the states of Nevada and Wyoming.

Increasingly, institutions of higher education offering education degrees are considering ways to incorporate microcredentials into their programs. For example, at Buffalo State University's International Graduate Program for Educators, multiple microcredentials can be combined to yield course credit. In school districts where tuition assistance is provided to educators pursuing advanced degrees, this assistance can be used to offset the cost of credit-bearing "stacks" of microcredentials.

Our hope is that, in the coming years, more states will incorporate microcredentialing as an integral part of licensure, endorsement, advancement, and continuing education for educators. In our view, a system in which educators' demonstrated proficiency connects to their licensure will both modernize and elevate the profession. Taken together, the actions of school, district, and state leaders can have a huge impact on the success of any microcredential implementation. With thoughtful structures and systems in place, educators will feel supported, valued, and encouraged as they engage in meaningful professional learning.

Conclusion

We wrote this book in part out of concern regarding the use of microcredentials. Across our combined 100-plus years in education, we have seen plenty of new trends come across our desks. We've heard all the buzzwords, programs, technology tools, and acronyms—all the promises that will truly, once and for all, revolutionize education. Of course, few if any can be said to have done this—and we fear that, if implemented poorly and haphazardly, microcredentials could succumb to the same fate.

We believe that microcredentials offer the potential to truly elevate professional learning for educators. As a result, throughout this book we have focused not simply on "trying out" microcredentials, but on using and implementing them in a way that truly transforms teachers *and* learners. As educators navigate the complexities of schools and classrooms, professional learning should prioritize student outcomes through sustained, relevant, goal-oriented, job-embedded, and personalized experiences. Done well, microcredentials can align with all these principles. With proper leadership and support, educators can progress from "I get it" to "I tried it" to "I have evidence that it benefits my students." What better outcome than to elevate both teaching and learning while positively impacting the lives of students?

Appendix A: Microcredential Key Traits Checklist

Key Traits	Evidence for Adoption
Performance-Based • A microcredential reflects transfer of learning or application of skills in authentic and complex situations. One or more skill-based objectives are included that align with the rigor of the performance-based task(s). • Successful completion of the microcredential is based on evidence that the learner is proficient in the skill. Credentials are not awarded simply based on a time requirement.	
Contextual • Completion of the microcredential is based on evidence that a skill has been applied in the context of the learner's work. • Learners engage in active reflection on how the skills being applied influence their daily practices and ultimately their students.	

continued

Key Traits	Evidence for Adoption
Personalized • Responses to the prompt or task will be unique to each learner, reflecting the learner's context, background knowledge, and application of the skill(s). • A variety of resources is provided for learners, which may include open access readings (book chapters, articles, or blog posts), videos, podcasts, websites, and so on. Some "challenge" resources are included for learners with higher levels of readiness.	
Standardized • Although responses to learning experiences will vary depending on the learner, the microcredential provides clear expectations and guidance for the completion of tasks to limit variations in quality. • Assessors will be or have been trained in consistent and reliable scoring of microcredential submissions.	
Self-Directed • The learner selects and accesses resources and opportunities that will be helpful in preparing to meet the requirements of the task. • The learner determines the timing and scheduling for any job-embedded tasks, including the length of time needed to design and implement the task requirements (e.g., spacing out the teaching of two lessons to provide adequate time for reflection and revision). • Individual learners decide where in the curriculum or in the context of their work the skill is best applied so that the task can be completed in the most authentic, job-embedded way possible.	
Accessible • The microcredential is easily available and affordable. • The microcredential has a flexible completion timeline to adapt to the needs and resources of adult learners. • The microcredential is readily accessed. Evidence and feedback can be easily submitted and viewed regardless of the platform or learning management system used.	

Key Traits	Evidence for Adoption
Valid • The evidence to be submitted, the resources provided, and the descriptors in the microcredential rubric clearly align with the identified skill(s). • It is possible to derive the microcredential's skill(s) by reviewing the rubric criteria and descriptors. The level of rigor of the task aligns with the skill(s). • Evaluative criteria are specific and detailed enough for consistent scoring across submissions.	

Appendix B: Virginia Beach City Public Schools Social Awareness Badge Criteria

With your submission, please include a brief statement to frame the context of your learning environment, such as grade level, content area, and other factors that affect your instructional decision making.

Please provide the following for the evidence submitted:

1. Clearly label each artifact with the criteria it supports.
2. Name the specific *social awareness skills(s)* that align with the artifact.
3. Include a written metacognitive statement/reflection that explains *how* and *why* the artifact is a demonstration of the aligned criteria.

Note: A single artifact may be submitted as evidence for multiple criteria.

Educators who support students to develop and reflect on their **social awareness** skills in the classroom have the knowledge, skills, and dispositions to develop a supportive classroom environment, integrate SEL into academic instruction, and provide responsive explicit SEL instruction.
Criteria   Standards for this performance
Criteria 1: Supportive Classroom Environment   Evidence demonstrates that the teacher uses social awareness practices/structures that are inclusive and culturally responsive, build community, and foster belonging and emotional safety.

continued

Criteria 2: Integration of SEL and Instruction
Evidence demonstrates that learners are provided opportunities to develop and practice their social awareness skills as they construct content knowledge, make meaning of academic content, and reflect on how these skills connect to and affect their academic progress.

Criteria 3: Explicit SEL Instruction
Evidence demonstrates that explicit instruction provides students opportunities to cultivate, practice, and reflect on developmentally responsive social awareness skills. Include a written justification of *how* your evidence supports the SEL strengths and needs of the students you teach.

Source: Virginia Beach City Public Schools. Used with permission.

Appendix C: Microcredential Criteria Checklist for Designers

Criteria (Key Traits)	Design Considerations
Performance-Based • A microcredential reflects transfer of learning or application of skills in authentic and complex situations. One or more skill-based learning targets are included that align with the rigor of the performance-based task(s). • Successful completion of the microcredential is based on evidence that the learner is proficient in the skill. Credentials are not awarded simply based on a time requirement.	_ Do the **skill(s), learning targets,** and **success criteria** go beyond knowing or understanding to require application of a skill in an authentic situation? _ Are the **learning targets** clearly aimed at proficiency rather than compliance in completing assignments? Is the **grain size** of the learning target appropriate for a microcredential? _ Will the required **evidence** provide sufficient information to indicate proficiency in the skill (i.e., are the learning targets, success criteria, and evidence aligned?)
Contextual • Completion of the microcredential is based on evidence that a skill has been applied in the context of the learner's work. • Learners engage in active reflection on how the skills being applied influence their daily practices and ultimately their students.	_ Does the grain size of the **learning target** make it doable for most educators in most settings? _ Can the required **evidence** be collected in the course of the educator's daily work? _ Does the required **evidence** include purposeful **reflection** by the educator?

continued

Criteria (Key Traits)	Design Considerations
Personalized • Responses to the prompt or task will be unique to each learner, reflecting the learner's context, background knowledge, and application of the skill(s). • A variety of resources is provided for learners, which may include open access readings (e.g., book chapters, articles, or blog posts), videos, podcasts, websites, and so on. Some "challenge" resources are included for learners with higher levels of readiness.	__ Is the **task** applicable to a variety of settings, content areas, and grade levels, *or* are there multiple tasks from which to choose, *or* does the educator design the task? __ Is the **task** open-ended enough to accommodate a variety of approaches or responses that demonstrate proficiency? __ Are **learning resources** provided in a way that allows educators some degree of choice in how they prepare for the task?
Standardized • Although responses to learning experiences will vary depending on the learner, the microcredential provides clear expectations and guidance for the completion of tasks to limit variations in quality. • Assessors will be or have been trained in consistent and reliable scoring of microcredential submissions.	__ Are the **success criteria** clear and specific enough to allow for reliable assessment of **evidence**? __ Is required **evidence** described in such a way that it is likely to demonstrate proficiency when warranted and not demonstrate proficiency when not warranted?

Criteria (Key Traits)	Design Considerations
Self-Directed • The learner selects and accesses resources and opportunities that will be helpful in preparing to meet the requirements of the task. • The learner determines the timing and scheduling for any job-embedded tasks, including the length of time needed to design and implement the task requirements (e.g., spacing out the teaching of two lessons to provide adequate time for reflection and revision). • Individual learners decide where in the curriculum or in the context of their work the skill is best applied so that the task can be completed in the most authentic, job-embedded way possible.	__ Is the **task** constructed so that it can be completed at a time and over a duration of the educator's choosing? __ Are **learning resources** readily accessible before, during, and after the educator engages with the task?
Accessible • The microcredential is easily available and affordable. • Microcredentials have a flexible completion timeline to adapt to the needs and resources of adult learners. • The microcredential is readily accessed. Evidence and feedback can be easily submitted and viewed regardless of the platform or learning management system used.	__ If a fee is charged for the microcredential, is it affordable? __ Is the microcredential posted in a place where it is readily available to educators and assessors? __ Is the process for external assessment (if applicable) transparent and timely? __ Is the platform or learning management system user-friendly for viewing, submitting, and receiving feedback?

continued

Criteria (Key Traits)	Design Considerations
Valid • The evidence to be submitted, the resources provided, and the descriptors in the microcredential rubric clearly align with the identified skill(s). • It is possible to derive a microcredential's skill(s) by reviewing the rubric criteria and descriptors. The level of rigor of the task aligns with the skill(s). • Evaluative criteria are specific and detailed enough for consistent scoring across submissions.	___ Are the learning targets, success criteria, task, and evidence closely aligned?

Appendix D: Annotated Microcredential

In the left column are elements from a microcredential on building classroom community. In the right column, we explain how the design of each of these elements aligns with the key traits of microcredential adoption and design outlined in Chapters 1 and 3.

Microcredential Elements	How the Elements Align with the Key Traits
Skill and Learning Targets	
Cultivate a learning environment where a strong sense of community contributes to learning. • Identify and apply a variety of community-building strategies that help learners feel safe and confident articulating their perceptions and needs with one another. • Can create a learning environment in which individual differences are embraced and valued. • Recognize connections between students' sense of belonging and their ability to learn.	In this example, the skill is broad and the grain size large. The bulleted learning targets describe the specific competencies that are a focus of this microcredential, establishing parameters that clarify this microcredential's specific competencies and grain size. Note that these competencies are *performance-based;* they describe actionable skills the educator can demonstrate in an authentic context (the classroom).

continued

Microcredential Elements	How the Elements Align with the Key Traits
Part 1: Pre-Reflection with Evidence and Success Criteria	
Pre-Reflection Questions Answer these questions in a written narrative of approximately two pages to provide a sense of your current understanding and use of this skill. There are no right or wrong answers; instead, the answers help provide context for your work on this microcredential. • Supply a *very brief* description of your community, grade level, content area, and any other aspects of your teaching assignment that provide context for this microcredential. • How does a classroom community where students feel safe and confident lead to a sense of unity in a classroom? • How can an environment where individual differences are valued contribute to deeper learning? • Are there students in your classroom or school who may not feel a sense of belonging? How does this manifest itself in day-to-day interactions? *Evidence:* Submit your written narrative. *Success Criteria* • The response addresses all questions. It demonstrates some understanding of classroom community and its relationship to learning. Examples and observations support this understanding. • The response is detailed enough for the reader to be familiar with the teacher's current context and understanding of building classroom communities among diverse students. • The response is clear and coherent.	We have found pre-reflection questions to be useful. In cases where evidence will be examined by external assessors, the responses help to understand the educator's prior experience or context. The questions also invite the educator to reflect how the skill impacts student learning, including in their own context. Focus questions can also enable an assessor (or a coach or colleague if guidance is being given) to provide early feedback that helps educators refine their thinking and direct their efforts toward the learning targets. The success criteria form the basis of a rubric. The type of rubric chosen (e.g., single-point, multi-point, holistic, analytical) and the way it is used will determine the extent to which the microcredential is *valid*. Our microcredentials employ a single-point rubric (meets criteria/doesn't meet criteria). Assessors provide descriptive feedback on each of the success criteria, citing evidence that supports their rating. See Chapter 4 for information on how to maximize validity.

Microcredential Elements	How the Elements Align with the Key Traits
Part 2: Task with Evidence and Success Criteria	
1. Based on your assessment of where your students are now, select no more than four classroom strategies or protocols that can be used to build community, help students interact positively with peers who are different from themselves, and enhance learning. Consider strategies like the ones from the optional learning resources in this microcredential (e.g., class meetings, acts of kindness). Use a chart like the one below to explain how each strategy can lead to a greater sense of belonging or community and what evidence of this you might see or hear in your classroom as the strategy is being implemented. 	Strategy	How It Can Build a Sense of Belonging or Community	What I Would Hope to See or Hear in My Classroom
---	---	---
		| 2. Plan a series of lessons in which students learn one of your selected strategies, practice it, receive feedback, and then apply it as they are learning subject-area content. For example, implementing morning meetings requires at least one session in which the process is introduced and lessons in which students practice ways of interacting in morning meetings with teacher (and perhaps peer) feedback. Once students are accustomed to the format, content can be embedded when appropriate (see the articles in your optional learning resources for examples). 3. Select two of your lesson plans: one in which you provided instruction, practice, or feedback in the strategy itself, and one in which your students applied the strategy or skill after practicing and receiving feedback. Add comments or notes to these two lesson plans describing how students responded to or used the strategies.	These activities are designed to ensure that the microcredential is *contextual*. They require the educator to demonstrate the learning targets in the course of daily practice, embedding these activities within regular instruction. Activities are open-ended enough to make the microcredential applicable in a variety of grade levels and instructional settings. In this example, educators begin by selecting strategies that are relevant in their specific context; they can *personalize* the activity to fit their learning needs and the needs of their students. Though educators may personalize the activities, approaching them in different ways, evidence will be assessed using a *standardized* approach. Success criteria are specific and descriptive enough to be *valid* and are qualitative in nature; that is, they describe the features of the educator's evidence rather than simply providing a checklist of tasks completed.

continued

Microcredential Elements	How the Elements Align with the Key Traits
4. Record a lesson in which students are using the strategy. Select a five- to seven-minute video clip that illustrates students applying the strategy after practice and feedback. If your video includes identifiable students, ensure that you are following your school's privacy policy. 5. Conduct a survey of all students or short interviews with two or three students whose levels of engagement or sense of belonging are likely not the same. Regardless of which format you choose, focus on understanding students' perceptions of (1) what they learned or what changed about their perceptions of others and (2) what they may notice about the culture of the classroom as a whole when the new strategy is in place. *Evidence* - Submit the chart that explains how each strategy can lead to a sense of belonging or community and the evidence you might see or hear in your classroom. - Submit the two lesson plans described in Activity 3 above, ensuring that you have added comments or notes to the lesson plans to describe how students responded to or used the strategies. - Submit the five- to seven-minute video described in Activity 4 above. - Submit the feedback from students described in Activity 5 above. The submission may be in the form of student responses to the survey or transcripts, audio, or videos of the short interviews. Submissions should not exceed seven minutes total. *Success Criteria* - The strategies in the chart are appropriate for students' developmental levels and context. It is clear from the explanation that the selected strategies are intended to lead to a sense of belonging or community as described in the learning targets.	

Microcredential Elements	How the Elements Align with the Key Traits
• One lesson plan emphasizes instruction in the strategy; the other emphasizes enabling students to apply the strategy. • Annotations/notes reveal that the teacher is observing students' responses and interactions and noting how they relate to a sense of belonging and community building. • The strategy being used by students in the video aligns with one of the lesson plans submitted and demonstrates students applying the strategy after practice and feedback. • Student feedback in the interviews or survey shows what students learned or what changed about their perception of others as well as what they noticed about the culture of the classroom as a whole when the new strategy was in place.	
Part 3: Post-Reflection with Evidence and Success Criteria	
In a brief narrative of approximately three pages, please respond to the following questions: • Return to the chart you constructed in Activity 1 and review the comments you made in the third column for the strategy you implemented. Compare and contrast your actual observations of students to what you hoped to see and hear, providing any insights you have about the similarities or differences. • Describe any ways in which your community-building strategy impacted student learning. • What is a community-building challenge you expect going forward, and how might you plan to address it? • How will this experience influence your next steps in community building that leads to deeper learning?	As we mentioned in Chapter 1, we believe that reflection is an important part of professional learning. These questions are designed to guide the educator's thinking about how working to develop the competencies described in the learning targets impacts classroom community, student learning, and future professional practice. Each educator will experience the microcredential differently, even though all will demonstrate the same success criteria. This further illustrates the balance in the microcredential between *personalization* and *standardization*.

continued

Microcredential Elements	How the Elements Align with the Key Traits
Evidence: Submit your written narrative. *Success Criteria* • The response addresses all of the reflection questions in enough detail for the reader to follow the teacher's thinking. • The response demonstrates insight regarding development of classroom community among diverse learners and its relationship to learning. • The response demonstrates that the teacher's reflection on this activity will be used to inform further learning and development. • The reflection is clear and coherent.	

Appendix E: Microcredential Reviewers Checklist

This checklist organizes feedback from external reviewers in order to help designers make final revisions to microcredentials before they are released for use. **This checklist is an example only;** these items should be adapted to reflect individual needs.

Checkpoints	Yes/No	Comments
Formatting		
Is the title in 14-point boldfaced Arial font?		
Are the narratives in 11-point Arial font?		
Introduction		
Does the introduction specify why this microcredential is important for effective practice?		
Does the introduction include links to current related research, articles, videos, or blogs?		
Does the introduction clarify whether the microcredential is part of a stack?		

continued

Checkpoints	Yes/No	Comments
Skill and Learning Targets		
Grain size: Is the skill significant and meaningful while being specific enough to demonstrate within a single microcredential?		
Are learning targets clear and specific enough that you can envision what the tasks or evidence might look like?		
Pre-Reflection		
Do the questions provide information about the teacher's current teaching situations, students, and demographics as they relate to the task?		
Do the focus questions elicit answers that give a clear picture of the teacher's current understanding/practice of the microcredential skill?		
Do the questions require reflection about the educator's current practice as it relates to the learning targets?		
Task		
Do multiple activities all contribute to demonstration of the learning targets?		
Can the activities be accomplished as part of most users' regular work?		
Does the task require a level of rigor or challenge that is probably beyond the scope of most beginning practitioners but well within the capability of most experts?		
Post-Reflection		
Do the reflection questions relate specifically to the skill and activities?		
Do the questions invoke thinking on how the completion of the microcredential influenced teaching practices and influenced student learning?		

Checkpoints	Yes/No	Comments
Evidence		
Does the task create evidence that clearly indicates mastery or nonmastery of the learning targets?		
Is the evidence that is required to be submitted an appropriate measure of skill acquisition?		
Are the specific artifacts/documents necessary for submission listed?		
Is the evidence able to be both personalized and standardized?		
Optional Learning Resources		
Do the learning resources legitimately help the teacher understand and prepare for the task?		
Are the learning resources widely available and free or easily affordable?		
Do the learning resources include a variety of formats (articles, videos, blogs, podcasts, etc.)?		
Success Criteria/Rubric		
Are the success criteria clearly derived from the learning targets?		
Are the success criteria detailed enough to determine successful mastery of the stated skill?		
Are the success criteria sufficient to demonstrate successful mastery of the stated skill?		
Can the rubric be used to assess evidence with consistency at an appropriate level of reliability?		
Alignment		
Are the skill, learning targets, tasks, and success criteria all aligned?		

continued

Checkpoints	Yes/ No	Comments
Please provide other comments, suggestions, or feedback you may have on any aspect of the microcredential:		

References

Aguilar, E. (2018). *Onward: Cultivating emotional resilience in educators.* Jossey-Bass.

Albemarle County Public Schools. (2021a). *Anti-racism policy.* https://www.k12albemarle.org/our-division/anti-racism-policy/policy

Albemarle County Public Schools. (2021b). *Our division.* https://www.k12albemarle.org/our-division

Alleman, J., Knighton, B., & Brophy, J. (2010, November/December). Structuring the curriculum around big ideas. *Social Studies and the Young Learner 23*(2), 25–29. https://www.socialstudies.org/system/files/publications/articles/yl_230225.pdf

Amabile, T. M., & Kramer, S. J. (2011). The power of small wins. *Harvard Business Review, 89*(5), 70–80.

Anderson, L. W., & Krathwohl, D. R. (Eds.). (2001). *A taxonomy for learning, teaching, and assessing: A revision of Bloom's Taxonomy of Educational Objectives.* Longman.

Camp, H. (2017). Goal setting as teacher development practice. *International Journal of Teaching and Learning in Higher Education, 29*(1), 61–72.

Cohen, P. N. (1995, August 1). Designing performance assessment tasks. *Education Update, 37*(6). https://www.ascd.org/el/articles/designing-performance-assessment-tasks

Council of Chief State School Officers. (2020). *Design, assessment, and implementation principles for educator micro-credentials.* https://ccsso.org/sites/default/files/2020-01/Micro-credentials%20-%20Design%20Principles_FINAL_1.pdf

Darling-Hammond, L., Hyler, M. E., & Gardner, M. (2017). *Effective teacher professional development.* Learning Policy Institute.

DeMonte, J. (2017). *Micro-credentials for teachers: What three early adopter states have learned so far.* American Institutes of Research. https://www.air.org/sites/default/files/downloads/report/Micro-Creditials-for-Teachers-September-2017.pdf

Dyer, K. (2018, March 29). What you need to know when establishing success criteria in the classroom. *Teach. Learn. Grow.* www.nwea.org/blog/2018/what-you-need-to-know-when-establishing-success-criteria-in-the-classroom

Ende, F. (2021). What's the key to sticky PD? *Educational Leadership, 78*(5), 38–43. https://www.ascd.org/el/articles/whats-key-to-sticky-pd

Evans, M., Teasdale, R. M., Gannon-Slater, N., La Londe, P. G., Crenshaw, H. L., Greene, J. C., & Schwandt, T. A. (2019). How did that happen? Teachers' explanations for low test scores. *Teachers College Record, 121*(2), 1–40.

ExcelinEd. (2019). *Micro-credentials: A game changing opportunity for states to support the professional growth of teachers*. https://www.excelined.org/wp-content/uploads/2019/06/ExcelinEd.Quality.MicroCredential.Brief_.June2019.pdf

Feldman, D. (2018). *Grading for equity: What it is, why it matters, and how it can transform schools and classrooms*. Corwin.

Finley, T. (2014, August 21). Generating effective questions. *Edutopia*. www.edutopia.org/blog/new-classroom-questioning-techniques-todd-finley

Freibrun, M. (2021, October 12). Using success criteria to spark motivation in your students. *The Teaching Channel*. https://www.teachingchannel.com/blog/success-criteria

Gallagher, J. J., & Ascher, M. J. (1963). A preliminary report on analyses of classroom interaction. *Merrill-Palmer Quarterly, 9*(1), 183–194.

Gamrat, C., & Zimmerman, H. T. (2021). Digital badging systems as a set of cultural tools for personalized professional development. *Education Technology Research and Development, 69*, 2615–2636.

Gonzalez, J. (2014, May 1). Know your terms: Holistic, analytic, and single-point rubrics. *Cult of Pedagogy*. https://www.cultofpedagogy.com/holistic-analytic-single-point-rubrics/

Gulamhussein, A. (2013). *Teaching the teachers: Effective professional development in an era of high-stakes accountability*. Center for Public Education.

Guskey, T. R. (2014). Planning professional learning. *Educational Leadership, 71*(8), 10–16. https://www.ascd.org/el/articles/planning-professional-learning

Guskey, T. R. (2021). Professional learning with staying power. *Educational Leadership, 78*(6), 54–59. https://www.ascd.org/el/articles/professional-learning-with-staying-power

Hattie, J. (2009). *Visible learning: A synthesis of over 800 meta-analyses relating to achievement*. Routledge.

Hattie, J. (2012). *Visible learning for teachers*. Routledge.

Hilliard, P. (2015, December 7). Performance-based assessment: Reviewing the basics. *Edutopia*. https://www.edutopia.org/blog/performance-based-assessment-reviewing-basics-patricia-hilliard

Jacob, A., & McGovern, K. (2015). *The mirage: Confronting the hard truth about our quest for teacher development*. The New Teacher Project. https://tntp.org/assets/documents/TNTP_Mirage_Executive_Summary_2015.pdf

Joyce, B., & Showers, B. (2002). *Student achievement through staff development*. ASCD.

Khattri, N., Kane, M. B., & Reeve, A. L. (1995). Research report: How performance assessments affect teaching and learning. *Educational Leadership, 53*(3), 80–83. https://www.ascd.org/el/articles/-how-performance-assessments-affect-teaching-and-learning

Krajcik, J., Schneider, B., Miller, E., Chen, I-C., Bradford, L., Bartz, K., Baker, Q., Palinscar, A., Peak-Brown, D., & Codere, S. (2021). *Assessing the effect of project-based learning on science learning in elementary schools*. https://mlpbl.open3d.science/techreport

Krathwohl, D. R. (2002). A revision of Bloom's taxonomy: An overview. *Theory into Practice, 41*(4), 212–218. https://www.depauw.edu/files/resources/krathwohl.pdf

Los Angeles Unified School District. (2021). *Los Angeles Unified fingertip facts 2021–22*. https://achieve.lausd.net/site/handlers/filedownload.ashx?moduleinstanceid=66505&dataid=109597&FileName=Fingertip_Facts_2021_2022_ENG.pdf

Luke, C., & Young, V. M. (n.d.). Integrating micro-credentials into professional learning: Lessons from five districts. *Digital Promise*. https://digitalpromise.org/wp-content/uploads/2020/10/Integrating-Micro-credentials.pdf

Marker, R., & Watson, R. (2018, November 1). Voice and choice makes the difference for teachers. *ASCD Express, 14*(7). https://www.ascd.org/el/articles/voice-and-choice-makes-the-difference-for-teachers

Marzano, R. J. (2007). *The art and science of teaching: A comprehensive framework for effective instruction.* ASCD.

McTighe, J., Doubet, K. J., & Carbaugh, E. M. (2020). *Designing authentic performance tasks and projects: Tools for meaningful learning and assessment.* ASCD.

National Education Association. (2021). *Classroom management.* https://nea.certificationbank.com/NEA/CandidatePortal/CategoryDetail_v2.aspx?Stack=CM

Norwalk Public Schools. (2021). *Our story and mission.* https://www.norwalkps.org/526499_3

Reeves, D. B. (2010). *Transforming professional development into student results.* ASCD.

Saavedra, A. R., Liu, Y., Haderlein, S. K., Rapaport, A., Garland, M., Hoepfner, D., Morgan, K. L., & Hu, A. (2021, February 22). *Knowledge in action: Efficacy study over two years.* USC Dornsife Center for Economic and Social Research, Gibson Consulting Group, and Penn State University. https://cesr.usc.edu/sites/default/files/Knowledge%20in%20Action%20Efficacy%20Study_18feb2021_final.pdf

Stiggins, R. (2005). From formative assessment to assessment for learning: A path to success in standards-based schools. *Phi Delta Kappan, 87*(4), 324–328.

Texas Education Agency. (2020). *Richardson ISD.* https://txschools.gov/districts/057916/profile

Utah Microcredentials. (2021). *Frequently asked questions.* https://www.uen.org/utahmicrocredentials/faq.shtml

VanderArk, T. (2013, December 26). What is performance assessment? *Getting Smart.* http://www.gettingsmart.com/2013/12/26/performance-assessment/

Virginia Beach City Public Schools. (2021). *About us.* https://www.vbschools.com/about_us

Webb, N. L. (2002, March 28). *Depth-of-knowledge levels for four content areas.* https://www.maine.gov/doe/sites/maine.gov.doe/files/inline-files/dok.pdf

Webster-Wright, A. (2009). Reframing professional development through understanding authentic professional learning. *Review of Educational Research, 79*(2), 702–739.

Wei, R. C., Darling-Hammond, L., Andree, A., Richardson, N., & Orphanos, S. (2009). *Professional learning in the learning profession: A status report on teacher development in the United States and abroad.* National Staff Development Council.

Wiggins, G. (2012). Seven keys to effective feedback. *Educational Leadership, 70*(1), 10–16. https://www.ascd.org/el/articles/seven-keys-to-effective-feedback

Wiggins, G., & McTighe, J. (2011). *The Understanding by Design guide to creating high-quality units.* ASCD.

Wiliam, D., & Black, P. (1998). Inside the black box: Raising standards through classroom assessment. *Phi Delta Kappan, 92*(1), 81–90.

Winchester Public Schools. (2021). *Winchester Public Schools fast facts.* https://www.wps.k12.va.us/Page/10607

Index

The letter *f* following a page number denotes a figure.

adoption of microcredentials
    adopt vs. design decision, 42–43, 43–45*f*, 45–46
        key traits as criteria for, 47–48
analytic rubrics, 58
Annotated Microcredential, 111–116
assessment
    of the credential, 80–81
    evidence element in design, 66–68
    in microcredential selection, 50, 52–53

book studies, 91

coaches, roles of, 89–90, 95–96
cohort model, 79, 90
costs, microcredentialing process, 22–23
criterion performance lists, 58

design, microcredential
    adopt vs. design decision, 42–43, 43–45*f*, 45–46
    evidence, examination of, 66–68
    reflection element, 65–66
    resources for, 61–63
    Richardson ISD, 41–42
    skills component, 55–57, 57*f*
    success criteria, 58, 59–60*f*
    tasks, 63–64, 64*f*
    Utah State Board of Education, 55

design process
    criteria checklist, 107–109
    designers in the, 69–70
    leaders in the, 68–69
    reviews, 70–71
    training in the, 70
districts
    microcredentials, advantages for, 4–5
    systems and structures to incentivize educators, 92–96
evidence element in microcredential design, 66–68

feedback
    element in microcredential selection, 50, 52–53
    examples, 82–84*f*
    for professional learning, 34–37
    quality, 80–81

grain size, 48–49, 56
guidance variable in microcredential selection, 50–51

holistic rubrics, 58

implementation, microcredentials
    accessibility element, 81–82
    assessing the credential, 80–81
    centralized approach to, 26–27

implementation, microcredentials (*continued*)
    cohort model, 79, 90
    feedback, providing, 80–81, 82–84*f*
    participant determination, 74–75
    piloting prior to implementation, 75–76
    supports, 77–80, 95–96
    timing, 84–85
    Virginia Beach, 73–74

leadership
    design process, 69–70
    district-level, systems and structures to incentivize educators, 92–96
    school-level, employing microcredentials as focal points for learning, 89–91
    state-level, 96–97
    teacher growth, guiding, 89
learner buy-in, creating conditions for, 33–34
learning resources element in microcredential selection, 51–52
microcredentialing
    costs, 22–23
    flexibility in the process, 22–23
    successful, requirements for a, 4
Microcredential Key Traits Checklist, 101–103
Microcredential Reviewers Checklist, 117–120
microcredentials
    advantages to schools and districts, 4–5
    defining, 14–15, 88
    essential components of, 15
    outline documenting teacher questioning skills (example), 15–18
    professional learning credits vs., 2–3
    purpose of, 55–56
    rationale for, 1–3, 87
microcredentials, key traits of
    accessibility, 22–23, 44*f*, 102
    alignment with traits of effective professional learning, 96–96
    checklist, 101–103

microcredentials, key traits of (*continued*)
    checklist example, 43–45*f*
    contextualized, 18–19, 43*f*, 101
    performance-based, 18, 43*f*, 101
    personalized, 20–22, 43*f*, 102
    self-directed, 22, 44*f*, 102
    standardized, 44*f*, 102
    valid, 23, 45*f*, 103

professional learning, effective
    evidence for, 11–12
    feedback in, 34–37
    goal-orientation in, 12
    job-embeddedness in, 13
    learner buy-in, creating conditions for, 33–34
    microcredentials alignment with traits of, 18
    personalization for, 13, 37–40
    planning backward from desired outcomes for, 27–30
    practice, creating opportunities for, 34–37
    as process vs. event, 12–13
    relevance in, 13
    theory of action, crafting a, 30–33
professional learning credits vs. microcredentialing, 2–3
reflection element in microcredential design, 65–66
review element in microcredential design, 70–71
rubrics for use with microcredentials, 58–59, 59*f*, 60–61*f*

schools
    employing microcredentials as focal points for learning, 89–91
    microcredentials, advantages for, 4–5
selection, microcredentials
    adopt vs. design decision, 42–43, 43–45*f*, 45–46
    Winchester Public Schools, 41
selection variables, microcredentials
    assessment, 52–53
    feedback, timing of, 52–53
    grain size, 48–49

selection variables, microcredentials (*continued*)
    guidance, 50–51
    learning resources, 51–52
    stacks, 49–50
    support, 50–51
single-point rubrics, 58
stacks, microcredential, 49–50
support variable
    in implementation, 77–80, 95–96
    in microcredential selection, 50–51

tasks, microcredential, 63–64, 64*f*
teachers
    career advancement, 93
    incentivizing, 92–96

teachers (*continued*)
    performance improvement plans, 91
    professional learning plans, 89
    stipends and raises for, 94
    supports for, 77–80, 95–96
    time for microcredentialing, 94–95
time, providing for microcredentialing, 94–95
timing microcredentialing, 84–85
training, responsibility for, 70

Virginia Beach City Public Schools Social Awareness Badge Criteria, 105–106

About the Authors

Eric M. Carbaugh, PhD, is a full professor in the Department of Middle, Secondary, and Mathematics Education at James Madison University in Harrisonburg, Virginia, where he instructs both undergraduate and graduate courses. As an educational consultant, he has worked with teachers and leaders at more than 100 schools and districts on a variety of topics related to curriculum, instruction, and assessment. In addition to several articles and book chapters, he is a coauthor of *Designing Authentic Performance Tasks and Projects: Tools for Meaningful Learning and Assessment* (ASCD, 2020), the quick reference guide *Principles and Practices for Effective Blended Learning* (ASCD, 2021), and *The Differentiated Flipped Classroom: A Practical Guide to Digital Learning* (Corwin, 2016). Carbaugh holds a Doctor of Philosophy in educational psychology from the University of Virginia, a master's degree in education from the University of Mary Washington, and a bachelor of arts in government and economics from the University of Virginia. He has teaching experience at both the elementary and secondary levels and serves as the journal editor and a board member for the Virginia ASCD chapter.

Laura McCullough, EdD, recently retired after serving nine years as executive director of ASCD's Virginia affiliate, where she was responsible for designing and overseeing a range of professional learning programs as well as outreach services such as innovation forums, VASCD's Profile of a Classroom, and a statewide network for new teachers. McCullough is active in policy and advocacy work, representing VASCD in the legislature and other policy arenas. She has taught at the elementary, middle, high school, and university levels, and has experience as an elementary principal and district administrator. She holds Doctor of Education and master's degrees in curriculum and instruction from the University of Virginia and a bachelor's degree in education with a mathematics concentration from Longwood University.

Meghan Raftery serves as the chief design officer of Edjacent, an educator design collaborative that provides resources for educators interested in leadership, collaboration, and entrepreneurship outside traditional K–12 school environments. As a freelance educator, Raftery also supports schools, businesses, and nonprofit organizations through curriculum design, innovation project management, and professional development. Her current work includes facilitating innovation initiatives for Virginia Beach City Public schools; designing and delivering curriculum and professional development for Defined Learning, a project-based learning platform; and providing project support for the CROP Foundation, a nonprofit that provides learning opportunities for students interested in the culinary arts. Raftery previously taught in elementary schools as a classroom teacher and gifted resource teacher and served as a curriculum coordinator and school/community partnerships coordinator. She holds a master's degree in teaching and curriculum from Penn State University and a bachelor's degree in education with a social studies concentration from Shippensburg University.

 **Ebbie Linaburg** retired after approximately 40 years in public education and continues to support education as a member of a local education foundation and as a board member of VASCD, where she currently serves as chair of the awards committee as well as collaborating on VASCD's microcredential initiative. During her career in public education, Linaburg taught secondary social studies and later had experience as an elementary assistant principal, a middle school principal, and the assistant supervisor for special education and student services. In the final years of her public education career, she served as assistant superintendent of instruction. Linaburg holds a master's degree in school administration from James Madison University and a bachelor's degree in American studies from the University of Mary Washington.

Related ASCD Resources

At the time of publication, the following resources were available (ASCD stock numbers in parentheses).

Compassionate Coaching: How to Help Educators Navigate Barriers to Professional Growth by Kathy Perret and Kenny McKee (#121017)

Creating a Culture of Reflective Practice: Capacity-Building for Schoolwide Success by Pete Hall and Alisa Simeral (#117006)

The Definitive Guide to Instructional Coaching: Seven Factors for Success by Jim Knight (#121006)

Demonstrating Student Mastery with Digital Badges and Portfolios by David Niguidula (#119026)

Designing Authentic Performance Tasks and Projects: Tools for Meaningful Learning and Assessment by Jay McTighe, Kristina J. Doubet, and Eric M. Carbaugh (#119021)

Digital Portfolios in the Classroom: Showcasing and Assessing Student Work by Matt Renwick (#117005)

The eCoaching Continuum for Educators: Using Technology to Enrich Professional Development and Improve Student Outcomes by Marcia Rock (#117048)

Making Teachers Better, Not Bitter: Balancing Evaluation, Supervision, and Reflection for Professional Growth by Tony Frontier and Paul Mielke (#116002)

The PD Curator: How to Design Peer-to-Peer Professional Learning That Elevates Teachers and Teaching by Lauren Porosoff (#121029)

Personalized Professional Learning: A Job-Embedded Pathway for Elevating Teacher Voice by Allison Rodman (#118028)

Principles and Practices for Effective Blended Learning (Quick Reference Guide) by Kristina J. Doubet and Eric M. Carbaugh (#QRG121056)

For up-to-date information about ASCD resources, go to www.ascd.org. You can search the complete archives of *Educational Leadership* at www.ascd.org/el.

ASCD myTeachSource®
Download resources from a professional learning platform with hundreds of research-based best practices and tools for your classroom at http://myteachsource.ascd.org/

For more information, send an email to member@ascd.org; call 1-800-933-2723 or 703-578-9600; send a fax to 703-575-5400; or write to Information Services, ASCD, 2800 Shirlington Road, Suite 1001, Arlington, VA 22206 USA.

WHOLE CHILD TENETS

1 HEALTHY
Each student enters school healthy and learns about and practices a healthy lifestyle.

2 SAFE
Each student learns in an environment that is physically and emotionally safe for students and adults.

3 ENGAGED
Each student is actively engaged in learning and is connected to the school and broader community.

4 SUPPORTED
Each student has access to personalized learning and is supported by qualified, caring adults.

5 CHALLENGED
Each student is challenged academically and prepared for success in college or further study and for employment and participation in a global environment.

The ASCD Whole Child approach is an effort to transition from a focus on narrowly defined academic achievement to one that promotes the long-term development and success of all children. Through this approach, ASCD supports educators, families, community members, and policymakers as they move from a vision about educating the whole child to sustainable, collaborative actions.

Building Educator Capacity Through Microcredentials relates to the **supported** tenet.

For more about the ASCD Whole Child approach, visit **www.ascd.org/wholechild.**

Become an ASCD member today!
Go to www.ascd.org/joinascd
or call toll-free: 800-933-ASCD (2723)

DON'T MISS A SINGLE ISSUE OF ASCD'S AWARD-WINNING MAGAZINE.

If you belong to a Professional Learning Community, you may be looking for a way to get your fellow educators' minds around a complex topic. Why not delve into a relevant theme issue of *Educational Leadership*, the journal written by educators for educators?

Subscribe now, or purchase back issues of ASCD's flagship publication at **www.ascd.org/el**. Discounts on bulk purchases are available.

To see more details about these and other popular issues of *Educational Leadership*, visit **www.ascd.org/el/all**.

2800 Shirlington Road
Suite 1001
Arlington, VA 22206 USA

www.ascd.org/learnmore

www.ingramcontent.com/pod-product-compliance
Lightning Source LLC
Chambersburg PA
CBHW060423010526
44118CB00017B/2341